# The Verbal Judo Way of Leadership

## Empowering the Thin Blue Line from the Inside Up

**GEORGE J. THOMPSON, Ph.D.**
**GREGORY A. WALKER, USASF (Ret.)**

**Looseleaf**
Law Publications, Inc.

43-08 162nd Street • Flushing, NY 11358
www.LooseleafLaw.com • 800-647-5547

**Library of Congress Cataloging-In-Publication Data**

Thompson, George J.
  The verbal judo way of leadership : empowering the thin blue line from the inside up / George J. Thompson, Gregory A. Walker.
    p. cm.
  Includes index.
  ISBN-13: 978-1-932777-41-3 (pbk.)
  ISBN-10: 1-932777-41-5 (pbk.)
  1. Communication in management. 2. Leadership. 3. Police administration. I. Walker, Gregory A. II. Title.
  HD30.3.T462 2007
  363.2068'4--dc22

                                                    2007009781

Cover design by Sans Serif, Inc., Saline, Michigan

# ABOUT THE AUTHORS

GEORGE J. THOMPSON, Ph.D. is the President and Founder of the Verbal Judo Institute, a tactical training and management firm now based in Auburn, NY. Doc Thompson, aka Doc Rhino, has an eclectic background, having taught English on the High School level (four years), English Literature on the University level (ten years), and served as a full and part-time police officer. Also a martial artist, he holds Black Belts in Judo and Taekwondo. Doc has created the only **Tactical Communication** course in the world.

Dr. Thompson has written four books on Verbal Judo, each analyzing ways to defuse conflict and redirect behavior into more positive channels. The Institute offers basic and advanced courses in the Tactics of Verbal Judo. Doc received his B.A. from Colgate University (1963), and his Masters and Doctorate in English from the University of Connecticut (1972), and he completed post-doctoral work at Princeton University in Rhetoric and Persuasion (1979). Widely published in magazines and periodicals, his training has been highlighted on such national shows as NBC, ABC and CBS News, CNN, 48 Hours, Inside Edition, LEETN, In the Line of Duty, and Fox News, as well as in the LA Times, NY Post, Sacramento Bee and other publications.

Aside from his well-known Police and Correction courses, Doc Rhino has designed special courses for educators, medical personnel, government and business employees, and the airlines. The Verbal Judo Institute has branch offices in Australia and Canada, and a national team of instructors who teach from coast to coast. Doc has taught over 175,000 police officers, and his course is required in numerous states across the country.

On a personal note, Doc and Pam are the proud parents of five-year-old Tommy Rhyno Thompson, and Doc, a survivor of throat cancer, has returned to active teaching. He also currently offers VJ training on the Internet, www.vjou.com. The publication of his doctoral thesis, *Hammett's Moral Vision*, is available in book stores, published by Vince Emery Productions, February 2007. You can browse Doc's website, www.verbaljudo.com or write him at VJI, Inc., 2009 W. Genesee St. Rd., Auburn, NY 13021. Office 315-253-0007.

GREGORY A. WALKER (ret.) graduated the Oregon police academy in 1997. He holds an advanced police certificate and is credentialed by Oregon's Department of Public Safety Standards and Training as a Content level instructor in 12 law enforcement disciplines including Verbal Judo.

His law enforcement awards and decorations include three Meritorious and two Distinguished Service commendations. He holds a degree in Social Sciences from the University of Alaska, Anchorage.

Honorably retired in February 2005 after 24 years of service in the special operations community with the Army's elite "Green Berets" and Rangers, Mr. Walker is a combat veteran of counter-insurgency warfare in El Salvador and most recently Iraq. His awards and decorations include the Washington Army National Guard Legion of Merit, three awards of the Army's Meritorious Service Medal, two awards of the Armed Forces Expeditionary Medal, both the Global War on Terrorism Expeditionary and Service Medals, Special Forces Tab, and two awards of the Combat Infantryman Badge (CIB).

His professional background includes three tours of Baghdad, Iraq as a Department of Defense high- risk security contractor in support of the U.S. reconstruction effort in that country.

Mr. Walker's previous books include *At the Hurricane's Eye - U.S. Special Operations Forces from Vietnam to Desert Storm*, *SEAL!*, and *Teammates*. He has written on law enforcement related issues for Jane's International Police Review and the Southern Poverty Law Center's *Intelligence Report*. Greg has appeared twice as a researcher and guest on CBS' *Sixty Minutes*, as well as on *The Today Show*, and as a subject matter expert on both the *History* and *Discovery* channels.

He currently lives, writes and teaches in the Pacific Northwest where he is also heavily involved in veterans' issues and affairs.

# DEDICATION

To Frank "Paco" Serpico - Whose never ending commitment to the hard right being done over the easy wrong on behalf of honest cops the world over continues to inspire, encourage, and motivate. Thanks to being there in 1974 when, as an unseen mentor, I needed you most, and for your wisdom, laughter, courage and kind friendship today.

Gregory A. Walker (USAF, Retired)

To all officers, everywhere, who 'do it right' because it's right, and never falter.

The Authors

And, most importantly, for my loving wife, Pam, and son, Tommy Rhyno, who have seen me through some arduous days – thank you!

Doc

# TABLE OF CONTENTS

ABOUT THE AUTHORS ................................................................ i

DEDICATION ............................................................................ iii

OVERVIEW
    THE TAO OF LEADERSHIP: THE HARD RIGHT ........ vii

CHAPTER ONE
    WHAT IS WRONG...AND HOW WE CAN MAKE IT
    RIGHT ............................................................................ 1

Chapter Two
    THE INGREDIENTS OF LEADERSHIP: ETHICS,
    VALUES AND RIGHT SPEECH ................................. 15

Chapter Three
    THE SUPERVISOR AS CONTACT PROFESSIONAL .... 33

Chapter Four
    THREE SURVIVAL TRUTHS FOR QUALITY
    COMMUNICATION ....................................................... 55

Chapter Five
    THE "HOOK DOWN" THEORY OF VERBAL JUDO
    SUPERVISION ............................................................... 67

Chapter Six
    THE FOUR LEVELS OF EXPERTISE ........................... 77

Chapter Seven
    YOUR COMMUNICATION PROFILE ............................ 83

Chapter Eight
    MOTIVATION AND REASSURANCE ........................... 105

Chapter Nine
    THE ART OF PRAISE ..................................................... 113

**Chapter Ten**
  DISCIPLINE AND CORRECTIVE ACTION .................. 121

**Chapter Eleven**
  THE ART AND GIFT OF PERSUASION ........................ 133

**Chapter Twelve**
  HOW TO DIAGNOSE A VERBAL ENCOUNTER ......... 145

**Chapter Thirteen**
  THE FOUR CRITERIA FOR ACTION ............................ 153

**Chapter Fourteen**
  THE TACTICS OF SUPPORT: L.E.A.P.S. ...................... 161

**Chapter Fifteen**
  LEADERSHIP AND THE ROLE OF TRAINING .......... 173

**INDEX** ............................................................................ 177

**COMMUNICATION PROFILE SURVEY (PULL-OUT)** ............................ 181

# THE TAO OF LEADERSHIP: THE HARD RIGHT

---

T his book has been a long time in the making. From the time I left college teaching to become a police officer, then a Reserve Officer, and then a full-time teacher of Verbal Judo for police, I have been listening to the patrol officers on the streets, here in the United States, Canada, and Australia. I have listened carefully to their complaints about management, to their hopes and desires for the job, and to their basic feelings about the society they serve. I have spent endless hours on the streets with these officers, and again and again I have been amazed by their skill and dedication. I have seen far too many officers grow cynical over time and hardened by what I see happen to them at the hands of management. So many officers enter the profession with enthusiasm and a real desire to excel in serving the public, only to end up waiting out their "Twenty," hoping for the day they can escape the daily pressures brought about by poor supervision and management. Many senior officers get to a point where they just do the bare minimum to get by, all vigor and desire gone. It has been sad to witness this gradual deterioration of morale and performance over the past twenty years.

The officer on the street is represented in this book first and foremost. My co-author and I describe what it should be, through the eyes of the street cop, as best we can. Taking as our basic premise that patrol is the most important, sacred job in police work, we have written a book for those who seek the privilege of supervising these officers. Some supervisors already do it right, and we take these officers as our models. Far too many do not do it right, either because they have never been properly trained to handle people, or they have the wrong attitude to start with and hence everything they do is doomed from the get-go! I know as a former supervisor of people that I needed right direction, I needed clear philosophy of guidance, and I needed specific tactics and techniques to handle the various and different people I was tasked to lead. Initially I had no such help, so I floundered, at first, and learned the hard way what I could have known from the start. I was lucky. Some never learn. Some continue to perpetuate the wrongs and hurt people as they do so. It needn't be this way.

My co-author, a combat blooded Special Forces operator and leader in his own right, has experienced similar challenges during his career in law enforcement at the patrol level.

Together we will tell the officer's story as we have experienced it over time. **Leadership is an art that begins and ends with honest, effective communication**. Communication with difficult people, under the Verbal Judo definition of such folks, demands consistency of focus and a knowledge of the strategies and tactics that actually work with such people. Brow-beating and daily intimidation does not work, although we see these approaches tried all too often! For years now Verbal Judo has been the premiere course in communication for police, and we now intend to educate supervisors in how to use these principles with their people. There are some books on Leadership that make good sense, but for some reason they have failed to make the proper impact. This is one reason for our rather blunt, direct style-we want to get the attention of those who have leadership responsibilities and power over others and encourage them sans "smoke and mirrors" to exceed their own expectations!

We first analyze **What Went Wrong**, showing that the present tendencies in supervision are wrong and destructive. We then define what we believe is necessary and that is people who possess right Ethics and Values themselves, and who can imbue others with those values. All good leadership begins and ends with a coherent philosophy of action, and we provide such a philosophy and show how to use it effectively with the troops. The good leader must be a **Contact Professional**, capable of being in contact with himself, his organization, his community and his troops.

We know that to lead people well, a leader must be willing to know more than those he serves. He must be an expert in what works and what doesn't, so we wish to make the supervisor smarter by teaching him the basic principles of effective communication. We then show how he can take this knowledge and apply it out on the streets with his troops. Particularly useful is our Personal Profile exercise, which teaches a supervisor what his basic underlying communication style is and how he can flex that style to relate effectively with the varying other communication styles of his people. Once the supervisor has a grasp of how he most naturally relates to others, we teach him the skills necessary to flex that style as he attempts to praise or discipline his subordinates. We also show how he can flex that style to relate more effectively with those who supervise him, so he keeps a good rapport with those above as well as with those below, including his immediate colleagues. We demonstrate how the supervisor can become a Conscious Competent in all endeavors within the department, a high level of skill that allows him to pass on his knowledge to his peers and troops.

Many books offer recipes on how to manage and supervise, but the primary strength of our book is we define the bottom line principles necessary FOR SUCCESS. For example, there are many ways to motivate one's troops, but the basic principle of motivation is to RAISE EXPECTATIONS. Whatever the supervisor does, his language and tactics must accomplish this end—raise the expectations of the officers that they can do more than they had thought. Similarly in attempting to reassure someone, the supervisor must project EMPATHY, or he will fail to capture his troops' hearts and minds. Additionally, many supervisors try to praise their troops, but because they do not know the principles of effective praise, their words become suspect and they eventually lose credibility. We define effective praise and show specifically how to deliver it, so it will be believed, and hence will motivate achievement rather than generate suspicion. The same holds true for the art of discipline or punishment. Often officers deserve to be reprimanded, even punished for wrong actions, but the **delivery** of that criticism is critical to a successful outcome and better officer. We show how a supervisor can praise or reprimand, even punish, while simultaneously raising morale—an impossible task without proper training and practice.

In the last third of the book we offer what is rarely if ever presented-how to **think** analytically and effectively. Much of a supervisor's job entails listening to proposals from others or offering his own for implementation. We define useful heuristics, ways of thinking, for handling verbal encounters (Chapter Twelve), for evaluating or proposing a policy or procedure (Chapter Thirteen), and for persuading others to first listen then endorse your point of view (Chapter Fourteen). Departments expect their supervisors to think well, but rarely offer effective training in analysis to help them. We offer this specifically, and any supervisor who reads our book will come away with an increased ability not only to handle people but to be more articulate and precise in his or her recommendations or evaluations of job related issues. A supervisor's success ultimately depends upon his ability to think **persuasively and analytically**, and *The Verbal Judo Way of Leadership* provides this training while also creating and giving strength to the "Thin Blue Line" from the Inside Up!

## CHAPTER ONE

# WHAT IS WRONG...AND HOW
# WE CAN MAKE IT RIGHT

---

Individual and organizational morale has plummeted over the years in many service professions, law enforcement being our primary example. The problem, we believe, lies in the mixed signals our professional and social organizations send out. They advocate the positive promotion of personal accountability, not a bad thing, then betray this laudable goal through endemic organizational compromise of their employees via poor execution of otherwise good policy and procedure. Our civil courts are dangerously overburdened with the litigation that comes from this systemic failure, not to mention the administrative haggling and brokering of employee unions and associations constantly representing their members' violated rights behind the scenes. Most often deals are cut as a result of these clogged and not-so-just "justice" systems, deals compromising professional ethics, morals, and standards in favor of protecting and promoting careers and interests well outside good personnel management.

21st Century police management is being gored by this frightening trend. For example, where before strict policies and procedures worked to protect the individual officer from superfluous accusations and complaints, today's professional police administrators and managers are teaching citizens they can directly attack an officer after the fact with little if any formal paperwork regardless of a department's standing policies. Furthermore, chances are excellent the officer will be at a minimum dragged into his immediate supervisor's office and read the riot act with little or no formal investigation conducted, much less one that is objective in nature.

For example, in one of our experiences an agency openly promoted citizens receiving something as routine as a traffic citation to challenge the issuing officer's effort or behavior by simply walking through the front door and "pitching a bitch." Management's concern was not for the well-being and integrity of its street cops and their actions but for management's public

1

perception of being intolerant of police wrongdoing at any level at any time. The result of this deliberate undermining of its own published complaint policy created a siege mentality on the part of those officers who were active traffic enforcement cops, and hence vulnerable to the whims of irritated traffic violators. These cops began to see themselves at the mercy of not only the violator, but also a management team willing to sell its officers out to make themselves look good both before and after the fact.

Interestingly enough, one officer with this department, a Verbal Judo graduate, began legally audio taping his traffic stops. Relying on his VJ training he taped his contacts with alleged violators and kept the interviews for 90 days before destroying them. When he began producing audio evidence that contradicted in traffic court not only the accounts and excuses made by the ticketed violator but also the unfounded complaints raised by his management team, the "complaint problem" evaporated in the distance between the customer service counter and captain's office!

What is the overall result of such questionable management tactics? Many officers and employees in both the private and public sectors today believe themselves hunted and inevitably doomed by their departments, agencies, and employers. This in the face of zero supervisory support and professional courage by those they rely upon to keep their best interests in mind as they go about their jobs. Too many police officers acknowledge they today overlook or refuse to respond to minor violations and offenses. This wrong behavior is a means of self-protection and a silent protest against management systems they believe are self-absorbed, vengeful, and intent on violating their own policies, procedures, and guidelines out of self-preservation. In professions other than law enforcement we see the same thing happening. When a low-level stock market employee will compromise his professional responsibility and personal ethics in favor of his job by sharing illegal information regarding a stock's imminent devaluation at the instruction of his boss, is it any surprise we have cops who will look the other way when someone runs a red light? We make no bones about it when we advocate that management is first and foremost responsible for quality, right leadership. Such leadership cannot help but produce right thinking and right acting employees if pursued vigorously with managers and supervisors who model such standards and do so with professional compassion, understanding, and thought.

In fairness, up until the 1970s, police departments were known to refuse to take complaints at all or would sweep valid complaints under the department rug. As a result citizens soon began to believe their concerns and fears were falling on deaf ears. And they were all too often right. However, society as a whole still universally believed their police could do no wrong. They believed a few bad apples or experiences could be-and perhaps should be-overlooked. If someone resisted the beat cop or called him a foul name, and the officer extracted a little "street justice" by thumping the offender, many good Americans would tell you the offender got precisely what he deserved.

With the advent of successfully argued police brutality lawsuits and criminal cases, and the ever-growing evidence of police corruption at all levels over the past three decades the public assumption that the police are always right and the offender always wrong has forever-thankfully-disappeared. Police officers and their administrations are now faced with 360-degree citizen suspicion and near-instant criminal and civil litigation. The same holds true in the private sector where a careless comment or innocent brush of the hand can land one in court and end one's ability to make a living in his or her profession. As a result of this backlash police departments and individual officers, as well as private sector employers and employees, have been forced to confront and deal with their need for certified, ongoing and verifiable communications and professional behavior training. This, in conjunction with a proactive, intellectually and ethically positive management atmosphere and environment that plays by the new rules with the best interest of the officer or employee at the forefront.

The profession of law enforcement is its own codified society. It has its heroes, its myths, its rules, regulations, traditions and ways of seeing the world it is required to function in. Part of what has gone terribly wrong with police management continues to be doing business "in the traditional way." Law Enforcement at the department level can change for the better only when its management does the same. Perhaps the most damaging negative historical behaviors that are driving good cops away from the job and leaving marginal performers in a position to rise to even greater levels of lackluster performance are cronyism and professional incompetence. When organizations and management systems partner with their communities and employee bases to cure these two cancers for the better, they can then deal more effectively and skillfully with the changing world of the greater society in which street cops have to work.

What, you ask, must we avidly seek to change for the better? First, current supervisors must change the way they relate to their officers. Such change can only take place if they first change how they relate to the job of policing society. As it is now the daily demand of routine policing (answering calls, issuing traffic citations, writing reports, appearing in court and interacting in a positive manner with those the officer provides his services to) is still not recognized as a proper profession in society's eyes. For this reason far too many law enforcement officers continue to be taught by their immediate supervisors that as soon as they leave the police academy routine police--street work--is something to get past as swiftly as possible so upward mobility in their departments and careers can be achieved. Woe be it the officer who wants to stay in patrol for the duration of his career. In today's mismanagement of police careers remaining a beat cop is looked upon with suspicion by anyone with rank greater than corporal. Why, the professional police administrator asks himself, is Officer Jones content to stay in uniform and work the street? More privately the professional ladder climbers who infest our police departments and agencies whisper amongst themselves: Why won't Jones play the promotion game like everyone else does? Climbing the promotion ladder as quickly as possible in police work is encouraged as the only way to receive proper recognition from the bosses downtown and hence better (safer?) assignments, pay raises and professional perks such as schools and training. Plus, society as a whole sees rank as the same as respectability. Ruthless promotion programs and unbridled advancement, not professional competency and human compassion, have become the twin gods of the American law enforcement career path.

My co-author experienced this early on in his career as a small town city cop. After successfully passing his probation he became eligible to compete for a suddenly open sergeant's position. When he made his intent to compete known, another candidate, who'd been with the department a few years longer and was religiously practicing the Art of Advancement, openly told his fellow officers that if his competition was chosen over him he'd quit and go elsewhere. The promotion candidate's widely articulated position on the subject was never challenged by his management team. While my co-author dropped out of the promotion board in favor of gaining more experience on streets, the other fellow was indeed advanced in rank despite his clearly negative attitude. The new sergeant would later become an important factor in three additional officers resigning and moving on, to include my co-author. Thus is the impact of retaining and promoting police careerists over qualified leaders and professionally committed law enforcement public servants.

Clearly a management system that encourages and rewards such thinking and behavior is as wrong-minded as it is destructive. **Protecting people from themselves and others intent on harming them or their property is a police mandate**. Those on the front line, meaning working the streets, are in fact the officers most valued and respected by the citizens they serve. If we think about it honestly, the "lowliest" street officer supervises hundreds if not thousands of people, daily, for eight to ten hours to 12 hours a day. No in-house supervisor does this, and if the truth is shouted from the rooftops many of today's police supervisors became supervisors specifically to avoid the responsibility "lowly" street cops thrive upon. Any routine call can be the street officer's last. On the street there is always danger, and real danger as opposed to an administrative officer's exposure to paper cuts, spilled coffee, or a crashed computer hard drive. Street officers, good street officers, must be independent in their thinking. They are challenged to be innovators, mediators, and street-savvy intervention experts. They must be correct in their performance and behavior at all times. For the weak police supervisor and self-serving police administrator, such officers are routinely marked as difficult to supervise, meaning control. Good street cops are fearless in word and deed. They do not tolerate disrespect from those who oversee their work, especially when they know who their boss is and how that person arrived at such a position. Because of the job they do daily, street officers are quick to perceive hypocrisy. They see right through the double-talk and politically correct mirage they are so often subjected to by middle and upper management. Their ability to sniff out and properly identify lame leadership is fine-tuned by their daily and often difficult contacts with the less than upright citizens they come in contact with during their shifts. Street officers know the job they do is important and of value to their society, but they quickly recognize from the way they are treated and what support they are given, or denied, by those above them what the real deal is. Sadly, it's the poor supervisor and administrator who retards good police work in a community, and diminishes the efforts of good beat cops in favor of maintaining their own false sense of self-importance and personal career accomplishment at any cost.

The street officer should be receiving the BEST training the department has to offer, and the most support, both in terms of equipment and positive reinforcement, that can be afforded. The newest patrol cars for example, should go to the officers using them to answer calls, not to management so they can go to lunch in style. In how many departments have we seen officers using trashed patrol units while their supervisors drive the best and the newest...or whichever SUV is the flavor of the day? We see this almost everywhere in our travels around the country's police agencies. When we visit with these organizations their management staffs often proudly claim the frontline troops are "our most important people," but very visible actions and quiet reports from the troops contradict this claim.

Case in point—one department, that we're aware of, spent a great deal of time and effort lobbying for a specific SUV to be purchased as a sergeants' car. After the vehicle arrived the sergeants guarded it jealously, even when it became clear the vehicle was going to be pressed into service when a sergeant wasn't on duty or a fleet patrol car was in the shops. The sergeants banded together and presented their views as to why patrol officers shouldn't be allowed to drive "their" SUV. Management concurred and the expensive and well-equipped vehicle then sat unused in the department parking lot whenever a sergeant was not working. Some months later the vehicle was badly damaged during the execution of a driving maneuver the SUV was not designed to safely conduct. The driver? A sergeant. The accident investigation allowed he was not responsible for the accident nor the ensuing damages to the vehicle. The result of all this was an ongoing joke in the ranks regarding their sergeants' ability to roll patrol vehicles...vehicles badly needed on the street whether driven by supervisors or patrol officers. Leadership in action? Not hardly!

Police officers should be selected and trained to work the streets, not the offices. They should receive the best training in the law, tactical communications, patrol tactics and techniques, crime scene analysis, evidence gathering and protection, courtroom testimony, self-defense, crisis negotiation, report writing, emotional survival, and enhanced supervision/strategic planning to include leadership that a department's budget can allow. Once on the streets, they should be carefully mentored, supervised, and developed not only during their probationary status but throughout their careers. Cops must be meaningfully and appropriately rewarded for thoughtful initiative and productive activity. Good street work is an art, not merely a series of field training officer-graded tasks. Officers must be imbued with this idea from the beginning of their careers. Officers need to believe that being on the street is "where it's at." That they are doing the real work of the department for the community, and whether in uniform or plainclothes, the street officer is the elite member of the team regardless of other specialty duties or assignments a department may offer.

Strangely enough, John Q. Citizen already believes this about the cop on the beat. What he values the most about the police is "Having my calls answered quickly and efficiently, and getting the service I need right now from a good cop!" He will *not* tell you his most immediate concern when calling the police is to chat with Chief What's-His-Name, or to explain the same thing several times over to some professional mid-level chair warmer sitting safely behind his all-too-neat desk. Successful, productive *contact* with the police is what a citizen values. Quality contact. Contact that results in near immediate action in some form delivered in a professional and knowing manner. Contact that sees their needs evaluated, repackaged, explained in simple terms and with clarity, and then met with a lawful, fair resolution. Officers deserve to be trained and rewarded for being *contact professionals*, capable of **Initiating** quality contact, sometimes with people who may not desire such contact or recognize it when offered. **Maintaining** quality contact even when an irate or upset citizen tries to break it off, and **Using** quality contact to resolve dangerous and explosive situations in as peaceable a manner as possible, must be the primary goal of every department's training program and senior leadership team. Officers who can deliver quality contacts on a daily basis for 20+ years are truly *Peace*

*Officers* and they merit our praise and their department's ac-knowledgment. Indeed, they are the "operators" of our trade, the ones who do the work, and for this they should be well paid, highly valued, and treated with dignity and respect.

But in many cases they aren't. In fact, such officers are seen by tradition bound, self-serving supervisors and upper manage-ment paper pushers as disruptive and threatening. Once identi-fied, today's police management system seeks these officers out and grinds them down, or pushes them out the door to another department or another career field. American law enforcement today is fearful at the top. Fearful of doing the hard right over the easy wrong on behalf of their communities and departments, fearful of losing their precious little rung on the fretful ladder of career progression in a field most other professions don't even acknowledge, and fretful of, at some point in time, being recognized for what they truly are as they scurry up the ladder of promotion and advancement, all those around them be damned.

Hard words? Yes. Tough to take? Only if you belong to the group of people described above. How often have I been invited to address a seminar of senior law enforcement professionals and offered during my opening statement that they have problems in their organizations...and the problems they have are seated before me? Some shift in their seats uncomfortably, others openly glare and scowl and appear to be reaching for the sidearm they stopped carrying after making captain. They know who I am talking about, and they know they have been recognized. The feel-good, pat-on-the-back luncheon they were treating them-selves to at their communities' expense suddenly became an indictment of all they hold dear and true.

Along with the abject and costly failure of so-called modern police management to recognize and support the professional street officer, is its slavish addiction **to promote those who work the street on the basis of how lousy a street cop they are**. If we grant notable exceptions, and certainly there are some, what is often the case is that an officer will fail to measure up to the rough and tumble world of beat cop work. His reward for this failure is promotion to a supervisory position. In return for taking him or her out of harm's way (being in management, he is told, will prevent him from doing further harm to the General Public), the newly promoted marginal performer is now expected to provide much needed internal political support to those in administration...this for saving his incompetent behind. The lesser officer will now supervise the street cops who knew from the beginning he was a detriment. If there was no professional respect for him as a street cop it is certainly true the newly promoted marginal performer will have no respect coming to him as a supervisor. Without such respect a supervisor in any organization is lost! Those who gain their rank in this manner become more fearful and angry than they perhaps were to begin with, and they aim this fear and anger toward those who know them for what they aren't. Make no mistake! Lousy supervisors KNOW how weak they are and how their professional acumen is perceived by peers and citizens alike. A department that promotes such an officer does he or she a disservice—*the officer will never be successful*—and likewise it does a crippling disservice to those who must work under the flawed supervisor's nominal control. Worse, such a management team reveals its own weaknesses and prejudices, if not ignorance, no matter how cleverly the promotional testing and interviews are arranged. Cops are trained to detect deception. Street cops will detect and react appropriately to any administrator who becomes a bully. Such a person is truly the victim of his or her own system of management, beginning with who he promotes and why. In many cases such senior administrators find themselves asked to move on once the damage they do becomes unforgivable. Their route becomes a steady downhill spiral to positions on departments that are small, unsophisticated, and often unable to hire/retain healthy, positive law enforcement management professionals to begin with.

The evil twin of this common tactic is the promotion of those who are "liked" by key individuals in management. Often, being "liked" means the officer is a Yes Man, someone who can always be counted on to go along with the program of the moment. The Yes Man never makes the mistake of giving bad news to his superiors. He never challenges their perception of what may or may not be occurring inside the department or out on the street. He believes, and then comes to enforce, the ancient dictum that the messenger is always killed, as many were in olden times by weak or tyrannical kings. Strong leaders value straightforward thinking and commentary because it challenges them to reevaluate their positions. The reevaluation process can save them from making egregious blunders! Those who leave the

truth telling to others hoping that by doing so they protect themselves, often go nowhere in healthy departments. In unhealthy
departments they rise to positions of power. Being agreeable,
meaning compromising one's self in order to get ahead or to avoid
being identified as less than supportive of the unhealthy management team, is considered by such individuals to be the mark of a
"team player." It is not. In law enforcement it is the signature of
an ethically dishonest officer. It is the trademark of the officer
who believes it is permissible to lie if he or she is not under oath.
It is the germ of the cancer that today permeates our law
enforcement community and it is killing the proud profession of
law enforcement just as surely as a bullet takes the life of a cop
on the job.

In all arenas, **great leaders listen to and respect their
subordinates, particularly the frontline people, the
"grunts," the operators**. What has gone so terribly wrong in
police work is leadership's failure to do just this! The best ideas
have always come from the people closest to the work at hand,
regardless of how harsh or bluntly put these ideas are delivered.
We can send our supervisors to all the management retreats and
leadership seminars available, and still experience failure at all
levels of leadership. This unless we first reinvest in our men and
women who do the important work as street cops and street
supervisors. Make a note! Too many "retreats" and seminars have
become thin excuses for drunken gatherings away from home by
our police supervisors and managers. These paid for by the very
citizens who are supposed to benefit from such affairs. Fooling the
public by slipping away to party with one's peers is dishonest, and
more folks than we would like to imagine know what really goes
on when you or your management team is supposed to be in class.
Those who abuse such potentially positive building blocks in their
supervisory career should be warned once, and then demoted. If
it happens again they should be terminated. Hard to do? Not if
you're truly a leader!

We should pay the experienced and wise street officer to stay
on the street, as long as he physically can, so his or her wisdom
can be passed on to new and less experienced officers. If he wants
to come off the street and supervise, then we must carefully
evaluate why he's made such a decision and then help him
achieve his goal. We must elevate our vision of the job of policing,
and reaffirm quality management at every level!

You may be reading this and saying to yourself, "My department already does this!" If so, we are truly happy for you! But, how many officers and departments can honestly assert this? Few. For example, think of how many departments have Field Training Officers (FTO's) with only two and three years of experience. Two decades ago it was the rule to have new officers trained by accomplished street officers with 15-20 years of experience. Today we hear of FTOs just past their probationary status being allowed to train newly graduated probationary officers. How did they rate such an important position within their department? My own experience tells me it takes at least five years of street work to make a seasoned officer, and this is in a busy sector or division. Well-meaning though these younger FTOs may be they simply do not have the experience to or the maturity to create new officers. Inexperience breeds mistakes, and those who are inexperienced and then chosen to teach will create poorly trained and motivated cops who will attract lawsuits and complaints like a magnet!

Why, in many cases, has the older and more mature officer been replaced in this critical role...which is the first formal line of leadership and supervision for the street cop? **Make a note! Too many departments do not regard extended street experience as real wisdom**. To be sure, some officers who have been on the job twenty years really only have one year repeated twenty times. They don't learn, won't learn, or can't learn. Over time they become inflexible and incapable of adjusting to the changing demands of policing. These people should supervise no one. In fact, they probably never should have been hired in the first place. But, many departments do have seasoned officers who have 5, 10, 20 years of valuable street experience, and these are the cops who should be the FTO's for the new generations falling into line behind them.

So why aren't they? **Many older, experienced officers do not want to be FTO's because it is a lot of work and responsibility. It also carries no great esteem within most departments**. This is because too many departments have watered their FTO programs down with inexperienced officers and favored department "pets." Fearful and often failed senior police administrators seek to fill the FTO positions with those who owe them, and therefore those who will "teach" new officers the importance of serving a flawed and failed management system. Hard-nosed street cops are not sought to fill a failed leadership's most important position in a department's internal structure, that of the FTO. Instead, all too often, such positions are given to those who bend over the furthest when the mighty pass by, and who can be counted on to curry favor instead of encouraging proficiency.

Often the FTO role carries no perks and little extra income, so it is a hassle many who should be FTOs feel they do not need. Viewed correctly, the Field Training Officer is the third most important job in the department, following fieldwork and patrol. FTOs single-handedly create the future of any department. They mold young men and women into young peace officers and then Peace Warriors. By doing so they set the tone for policing on the street. Proud and competent FTOs have great power because the young officer looks to them for guidance and will heed their advice over any other source. If the Academy teaches something to the rookie and the FTO later says it's hogwash, the rookie will believe the FTO. Such people wielding this much influence should be our best, our brightest, our most tested, and our most experienced. The FTO should be a position sought after and well-rewarded. It is also where we should be finding our best-qualified potential supervisors and managers for later on down the promotional road.

And finally, if all the above were not enough, add the wrong-headed **"business mentality" of present-day police work and you will fully understand why morale is so low**. This is why your department's good cops are leaving for other departments providing even a glimmer of better working conditions and professional hope! At the top end of a department, there are admittedly business concerns, budget and payroll being the two crucial ones, but where the real work is done, on the streets, the business metaphor when carried to the extreme is inappropriate and harmful.

Managers do need a way to hold their people accountable, and statistics and numbers are one way to do this. But HOW these stats are interpreted and used has become a major stumbling block in police work. For example, supervisors need to know the areas and "beats" their officers patrol so they can read the incoming stats appropriately. Officer #1 may be working in a high burglary area. Certainly his supervisor would hope to see on the daily log numerous Field Interrogations (FIs) and enforcement effort. Aside from answering calls, the proactive and effective supervisor would want to see his officers' time spent walking the alleys behind stores and businesses, shaking doors, checking locks, and talking with people in the area. Doesn't this just make good sense?

Officer #2 may be working an area known for traffic accidents and careless driving, so the effective supervisor would look for numerous speeding tickets, warnings, and traffic arrests. This form of proactive activity demonstrates his officer is responding to the most significant problem on his beat.

All this seems obvious, yet what happens over and over again is that incompetent, mean-spirited, leaderless supervisors don't know (or perhaps don't care) how to correctly evaluate the information they get from the street and then apply it toward enhancing, in a positive manner, the performance of the officers they are responsible for.

Officer #1 gets hammered by the idiot supervisor for not having enough traffic tickets for the month and Officer #2 gets hammered for not shaking enough doorknobs! You've seen it and so have we. It is killing us where good police work is concerned, and good police work is the only work that counts!

Another example. Some of the best community policing work is almost impossible to define according to stats and figures. True experts in the field of community policing acknowledge this. Statistics are only useful if the supervisor knows his people and the areas they work. Too many managers have lost touch with the street and with their officers. They fail to remember that quality police services cannot be defined by pie charts alone. I'll never forget talking to a West Coast deputy as he was getting ready for his shift. I had just finished a Verbal Judo basic course at his department. The deputy told me, "You know, Doc, you're right about management being a big problem. I just got my evaluation for the month and I got dinged hard for not having enough FIs and tickets.

"I lead this department in felony arrests and last week caught two bank robbers in the act. Not a word about that was in my eval! If all they want are stats, I can always go to the phone book and create twenty FIs for the month! It's ridiculous!"

What a shame! Police work is not a business, it is not a matter of slots and totals, and it never will be. It is a service, unique in its demands and equally unique in its means of measuring success and failure. The quality of the individual officer is **the** only crucial issue. As we will present later the only way for an immediate supervisor to measure and properly acknowledge the quality of work being done is to be in the field with the officer. With budget crunches and personnel losses soaring, we need to motivate, value, and hoard the good officers we have.

Make a note! Supervisors and upper level managers who would tell you and me they are in the same league as the guy who runs a private corporation (such as a fast food outlet) are **wrong!** If you want to be in business then hang up your badge and gun and invest in a hamburger franchise. Police work is service work! Service work is people work. And **cops** are first and foremost **people**. If you can't service your people as a supervisor or chief, you are slowly killing your department and therefore your community as a law enforcement professional. Hard words? Yes. True? Absolutely! Make you angry when you read them? What are you going to do about it then?

We must start with the **Right Vision** if we are to become true and respected leaders in the profession of law enforcement. The street officers are our *elite* corps. They are the foundation and the basis of a department's ultimate success. Let us commit ourselves to this premise, and let us change anything that does not conform to this premise. Only in this way can we field a strong, dynamic body of men and women who are capable and willing for 20+ years to fully protecting our citizens and providing them with the levels of long term service expected and needed for the duration of a career to be proud of.

CHAPTER TWO

# THE INGREDIENTS OF LEADERSHIP:
# ETHICS, VALUES AND RIGHT SPEECH

T
here are leaders working amongst us who inspire our confidence and instill, as well as nurture, enthusiasm for our jobs. We have interacted with a broad spectrum of such leaders whose everyday words and actions exude honesty, integrity, and a genuine love for the people they are responsible to. What makes them better? Character. They have the right stuff. They have trained themselves to be the walking embodiments of professional and personal **Ethics/Values**.

There are some of you who are perhaps not yet promoted but who believe you want to assume a leadership role in your department or agency in the future. There are those of you already in positions of authority and this chapter will reinforce what and who you have already become. And then there are those of you which this chapter, in specific, may clarify who you should be.

When we enter the profession of law enforcement we walk upon perhaps the most visible social stage in our society. Because the uniform, badge, and gun immediately makes us stand out in a crowd everything we *say* and *do* is translated as the desire and will of our community, city, county, state or federal government(s). As law enforcement officers we truly cease to possess an individual personality once the uniform is on. We become the embodiment of authority of the People under government. In this unique circumstance, **law enforcement officers are challenged to restrain their private feelings and personal opinions when on the job. This, while also modeling a public life of exceptional moral integrity and professional ethic.** How many of your professional and personal mistakes and blunders can be directly traced back to the power of an undisciplined tongue, or to a lapse in ethical or moral judgment?

There is the story of the police sergeant who, upon ordering one of his officers to write a report regarding the use of force during an arrest, lost his temper with the officer when the report wasn't written to his satisfaction. With a third department member present but unseen in the squad room the sergeant loudly swore at, issued allegations, and threatened the officer he was unhappy with and didn't particularly like. After the report was rewritten the offended officer quietly filed a complaint regarding the sergeant's behavior with the union. A memorandum from the third party who overheard the sergeant's tirade was submitted, as well. The officer then went to all those parties alleged by the sergeant as having witnessed the officer's claimed behavior regarding the use of force. One party denied ever being aware of the situation. Another stated his only reason for bringing the matter up with the supervisor was to let the officer in question know he may have—for a moment—become lax. "If I'd known he [the sergeant] was going to handle it the way he did, I never would have said anything!" the embarrassed officer confided to his peer. In the end, the primary officer involved lost all respect for his sergeant. This clearly was a direct response to the inappropriate and unprofessional manner in which his supervisor spoke to as well as treated him. We make this point time and again in our seminars and lectures on tactical verbal communications: our ability to verbally communicate is our most powerful weapon! It is likewise a two-edged sword, which can cut crucial ties of respect and support between us and our subordinates, as well as our own throats, if our words betray flaws in our character or ethics after the fact.

In this instance the supervisor crossed the lines of ethical behavior by behaving toward his subordinate in a manner that would never have been tolerated if the officer had behaved in the same manner on the street toward a citizen. He compounded his mistake by lying to the officer about which of his peers was supposed to be involved in the reporting of the alleged incident, and compromised himself and his department by ordering a report be rewritten to suit his version of the incident. The fact that he was overheard by another officer and that claims could be researched and either confirmed or denied resulted in a union complaint he could not counter. He went on to lose the trust and respect of no fewer than three officers! Finally, he failed to be a credible source for the correction of what may have been a weak link in the original officer's professional armor.

As a leader at any level in an organization your first concern must be your **ethical bearing**. The word Ethics comes from the Greek word **Ethos**, meaning "self." This is the Self as seen by others. For police officers this is your performing, or professional

Self. Ethics, or professional performance, is often presented in a far too complicated manner beginning at the police academy. However, at the Verbal Judo Institute we believe Ethics (or your professional performance) is truly a very simple concept to both teach, learn, and then model for others.

Ethics mean **you must be what it is you represent at all times, on or off the job!**

Yes, that's it.

Here's where many chiefs and supervisors, as well as street officers, make their mistake. The police represent law and order in our society. Therefore police officers must talk and behave lawfully and orderly when interacting with our society. If they represent Peace—which is why historically U.S. law enforcement professionals have been called *peace* officers—they then must act far more peaceably than those whom they are responsible for and indeed are paid to *serve.* Any level of supervisor, as well as a street officer, who swears or belittles or otherwise disrespects his subordinates or the people he comes into contact with is not performing in accordance with what he represents (Law and Order). Hence he is not ethical in the administration of his duties as a peace officer, much less a manager or supervisor of *peace* officers.

All too often those among us who have been selected to wear the gold distinction of rank and authority daily behave in ways that diminish their professional credibility, either behind closed doors or out on the street. At the **Verbal Judo Institute** we believe that **Showtime** *begins as soon as you put on the badge and leave your home.* Police managers and supervisors who backstab patrol officers or who routinely engage in the personal and professional destruction of a colleague are known and remembered by all officers. They are also most often the same people who did the same with citizens they came into contact with during their climb to leadership positions within a department or agency. Leopards seldom change their spots. Your reputation, whether *you* believe so or not, is the sum of what your peers and those who you contact on the street remember you as having said or done while under the authority of your department.

Don't believe us? Take a moment to think about how many current administrators, managers or supervisors you know or have worked with who today possess little no professional credibility because of what they have said or done in the past. Even more shocking is that these folks carry on as if they have no such past. They blunder through their workday wondering why they have no positive influence or effect on those they are supposed to lead and command. You hear them whining and complaining that their ineffectiveness in the department or on the street is the fault of someone else, or a collective of "someone else's."

In truth such individuals are lazy, brutish, and incapable of self-introspection and renewal. Such supervisory staff members routinely destroy good officers and violate the Public Trust every time they come to work. Their professional performance, if examined by an objective body, is often discovered to be fraught with errors and oversights. They cost their employers money at every turn and they rely heavily on the ancient art of rump kissing to maintain their positions of power and authority over their often-inflamed subordinates. They are those who give good cops a bad name, and they are too stupid to quit or retire until they have damaged a department sometimes beyond repair.

One senior administrator we are aware of had maintained his position for nearly a decade. Along the way the turnover rate for his overall employee base was roughly one certified officer a year plus a support staff member. His department's yearly union complaints were extraordinary in number for the size of the department. The union representative told us he was in awe of both the frequency of complaints filed against the department management by its own officers, and of the nature of the complaints, most of which were won by the officer/union. The senior administrator, rather than extend himself as a leader and seasoned professional, adopted a policy of turning everything that went awry over to the city's labor attorney and human resources director for action. In his mind they were there to fix his mistakes, or to assume partial responsibility for the mistakes he was in the process of making. No doubt thousands of dollars were wasted on legal opinions that in the end went nowhere, and hundreds if not thousands of city man-hours were exhausted conducting administrative procedures doomed to dead ends. This because one city official found it easier to misuse the system than to strengthen it by being the professional he'd been hired to be. His department and community suffered the loss of trained and experienced officers year after year with no one being the wiser as to why they were leaving and who was ultimately responsible. This same senior law enforcement administrator once told a subordinate regarding a respected administrative assistant who'd resigned after ten years of service to the department that, "She didn't understand that sometimes you have to compromise your ethics to do this job."

Ethics. Your consistent and public professional performance as a peace officer is directly tied to your ethics. Without this crucial bonding you, as either a leader or subordinate (and there is nothing wrong with being a good and trustworthy subordinate), cannot hope to possess or display professional credibility. And a cop with questionable professional credibility is a living, working liability to both his society and his department.

Once you lose your professional credibility in the field of law enforcement you are finished! You may not find yourself out of work but you will find your work out of favor. The word **credibility** comes from the Latin word "credo" meaning belief, or what people believe. Should we lose our credibility, we in fact lose the People's, or our community's belief, in what we *represent*, as well as *do*, on their behalf. Once belief in what you as a peace officer, supervisor or otherwise is lost, also lost is your *mandated authority or POWER* to act according to the law within our society. As a leader or supervisor, lose your officers' belief in you, or the Public's belief in you as a credible representative of Law and Order, and your ability to influence others (to bring order out of disorder, peace out of conflict, the truth out of lies) comes to an end. Sadly, too many departments maintain employees within their organizations who literally have no *power* to successfully execute their duties other than the badge on their shirts and the guns on their hips. In their departments and on the street and in the courts they are known to be, at worst, suspect performers. They lose their peers' respect, the respect of the people they were hired and swore to serve, and crucial cases at trial when the ethical soundness of the investigating officer is the only thing that can deliver a just conviction or acquittal.

If you are a manager or supervisor now, or a promising leader for the future, you MUST begin building your professional résumé and reputation (both which are performance-based) by curbing the natural tendencies of your mouth and behavior and becoming both careful and consistent about what you do in front of your supervisors, peers and your public. It is true in all walks of life that the past is never quite forgotten and our foibles are never quite forgiven. Still, our bosses, our peers, and our public do extend great rewards to those who recognize their shortcomings and actively seek to correct their faults. Begin today **to become who you must be** as a living symbol of ethical responsibility and behavior in the eyes of others…, which may not initially be what you have come to believe that a law enforcement professional is. How's that?

Hollywood has all too often created despicable mutations of the police for the sole purpose of entertaining society's worst conceptions about cops. In the real world of police work there are cops whose behavior equally scuttles the honorable reality of a cop's job and how he or she is expected to perform it. Ethics is the beacon of light that guides us to safety regardless of the storm we are faced with. Exceptional leaders define, then live, ethical lives, both on and off the job so as to constantly model, in a positive and dependable manner, what is expected of their subordinates under the same circumstances.

Bad cops are more often than not the result of bad police leadership.

How do you take the first step on this new path of professional excellence?

Be and be prepared to *act ethically* at all times. Federal and state law as well as department policy binds all peace officers to intervene when their managers, supervisors, subordinates and peers behave illegally or inappropriately. This is where leadership begins if you are a peace officer. There is no double standard for "us" and for "them." The "Thin Blue Line" between order and disorder, peace and conflict, truth and untruth cannot perform society's business if law enforcement officers behave as their society does. Peace officers must be infinitely better! The wrong reaction to witnessing a violation or crime by a fellow officer is to ignore it. This is the infamous *Code of Silence* that bedevils law enforcement. However, such "codes" are not uncommon in many other circles, particularly the legal and medical professions. But cops who practice such a code are universally condemned by our society and for good reason. Society simply expects more from an underpaid, under-trained, overworked, under-educated peace officer than it does from its lawyers, doctors, and politicians.

Over the years we have seen the horrors the *Code of Silence* has birthed from the west coast to the east, and from the north to the south. And it never seems to end. When chiefs, captains, lieutenants, sergeants, corporals, and line officers willingly encourage or participate in covering up the illegal or inappropriate activities of their brethren the *Thin Blue Line* disappears and chaos, both inside and outside of the department, holds rein. As a leader, or up and coming leader, you must live the truth that **ignored behavior is condoned behavior!** If you look the other way you involve yourself in this most basic level of professional corruption and conspiracy.

California P.O.S.T. stresses the study of Ethics in their basic academies. In these classes they teach officer candidates that a peace officer has the **obligation** to intervene in illegal or inappropriate conduct. California's P.O.S.T. instructors present three levels of officer initiated intervention: These are IMMEDIATE-DELAYED-ADVANCED intervention. In our studies and travels we've found the California model to be perhaps the most practical such model to clearly define and demonstrate the execution of responsible ethical performance for peace officers. This California model also suggests an implacable fact: we must **TRAIN officers** in ethical values and conduct and we must **insist on ethical conduct** at every level of a department.

## Immediate Intervention

This level of intervention requires an officer to take affirmative action to prevent a violation by another officer or officers. This level of intervention ranges from an officer stopping or restraining another officer from delivering an illegal blow or strike with his fists or his baton to saying the right thing at the scene that prevents planned or impromptu corruption or theft. Consider what might have occurred had but one officer so intervened in the 1991 police beating of Rodney King?

Yes, there is danger to such intervention. It puts you, the responsible peace officer and peer, in the spotlight. All too often peace officers in America fear the reverberations of taking this position. Sadly, they are taught to fear meaningful, ethical intervention more than civil or criminal allegation. And unethical chiefs, managers, and supervisors teach them this misbehavior.

We have been told had any one of the officers present during Mr. King's beating intervened he would have been "history" with the Los Angeles Police Department at the time. He would have first been ostracized by the management, then officer body and then driven from the department. We would like to believe this might not have been so. But we cannot, and neither do you if you've any time in law enforcement whatsoever. It takes courage to step in and act ethically, and therefore differently, than your colleagues. It takes the greatest commitment to personal and professional honor as a peace officer to stop an injustice at the hands of another cop. However, it is what you are hired to do. There are serious, career-killing risks to ethical behavior in police work. But the true leader, the true Peace Officer, does not run from these risks, although to fear them is certainly normal. Those who aspire to leadership in their departments at any level must behave and perform according to the higher principle of right behavior in conjunction with law, policy, and procedure. If you do there is no one who can stand against you either in or out of the courthouse. If you don't, then you begin the slow, slippery downhill ride toward being no better, and arguably worse,than those we call criminals.

I witnessed an example of immediate intervention while on patrol one night. Several of us responded to an open door call at a local jewelry store at 3:30 in the morning. We searched the store, found nothing disturbed. We called the owner to come and lock up his business. I and another officer saw a Rolex watch on the counter. It was somewhat hidden by some papers and trash. It had apparently been overlooked and left out as the business closed its doors for the day. A third officer stood nearby. We waited for about a half an hour, and I finally stepped outside to see if the owner might be arriving. When I came back in, I noticed the Rolex was gone. The officer I was with asked me in a whisper if I noticed it was missing. "Yes," I answered. He and I then knew the third officer had stolen it. The man I was with, a senior officer with 15 years on the job whispered to me, "It will reappear. Standby." He drifted over near the other officer and I saw him say something so quietly I couldn't make it out. Ten minutes later when the owner arrived the Rolex was back on the counter.

After we'd cleared I asked my partner what he'd said to the third officer we suspected had lifted the watch. He said, "I told him I had seen the watch and it needed to be returned...or an arrest would be made." That was all well and good but I was still concerned. "What do we do now?" I asked him.

He waited a moment then said "Nothing, just yet. But I now know I need to watch him very carefully. If he trips up again, he's gone. I also know I need to have an extensive chat with him about ethics, something the academy apparently didn't hit hard enough."

This incident took place in 1978. Today the offending officer probably would not be given a second chance. My last question for my partner that night was would he really have arrested a fellow officer if the watch had not been returned? He told me he absolutely would have. A cop who is or becomes a thief betrays all that the peace officer stands for. If you'll let a brother or sister officer get away with committing a criminal act, you should by rights allow the citizen to do the same. Worse yet, if you witness such an act committed by a fellow officer and do nothing, you yourself become a party to the act, with all the ramifications such association brings with it.

A cop who lies under oath, or during a disciplinary hearing or investigation, is ethically wrong, as well as a liability to all those other officers in a department. Consider this example. A woman was arrested for DUI by a Southern California peace officer as she left a Burger King drive-through window and went left of center on the roadway. The arresting officer performed street sobriety tests, which she failed. She was transported to jail by another officer while the arresting officer searched her car and stood by for the tow truck. During his impound search he found a cheeseburger in the front seat of her car and he ate it!

The next day after the woman was released from jail she picked up her car. She noticed her cheeseburger was gone. She went to the officer's department and complained he'd eaten her cheeseburger. She went as far as to present her receipt to the lieutenant taking the complaint. An investigation showed no cheeseburger had been entered on the impound inventory sheet. The officer was called in and asked if he had indeed eaten the cheeseburger. He denied doing so. The results of the investigation showed he was lying and he was subsequently fired! His department correctly determined if the officer would lie about hogging down someone else's cheeseburger, he would lie about other things as well.

Immediate intervention could have helped this officer during that brief period of time between his having to answer his department's questions truthfully, and then actually presenting himself to his superior to do just that. This ethical reminder could have come from a fellow officer, a supervisor, or even the person charged with finding out what occurred. A voice in his ear at the right time would have told him that no lie—or cheeseburger—is too small of an issue to get you righteously fired. Peace officers are not perfect and our Society, as well as our officers' employers, knows this. However, lying under oath or during policy mandated and guided personnel actions will always result in termination in a responsible department that carries out its investigations appropriately and in accordance with civil, criminal, and labor law as well as departmental policy and procedure.

Allow us to share a perhaps more sobering example of when immediate intervention is deliberately sidetracked, and when the violator wears gold on his sleeves.

A violent offender was being arrested one night. During the arrest the suspect began to fight the officers. This was not unexpected, as the man was well-known to physically resist arrest whenever confronted by the police. This time, however, as the suspect was taken to the ground the supervisor on the scene took out his baton and began to beat the man. Afterwards he told those other officers present that they would say nothing about this to anyone. His size, reputation for being a bully within the department, and rank had the desired effect. Nothing was said... until much later. In the meantime the suspect was taken to jail where he continued to fight. As he was being subdued the marks of the baton became clearly visible. However, no one knew, or would say, how he'd come to receive them. The suspect knew, and he loudly stated how the police had beaten him. Still, no one who knew what had happened out on the street would say anything at the time.

The suspect was convicted and did time. When released he returned to his bad habits but now he began carrying a gun. When asked why by a friend, who reported the conversation to a police officer later, the suspect said the police would never again beat him.

Unethical cops are bad cops. And bad cops get good cops killed in the line of duty by their unethical, possibly criminal behavior. Failure to intervene when intervention becomes necessary can lead to a fellow officer's death later on down the road. Think about it the next time you witness unethical behavior on the part of a fellow officer...then do the right thing immediately.

## Delayed Intervention

Delayed intervention occurs when an ethical violation has taken place and someone, the violator or another officer, steps in after the fact to make it right. The swifter such intervention occurs following the inappropriate behavior the more effective it will be. For example, an officer swears at someone during an arrest. It is delayed intervention if the officer goes back, after the event, and apologizes to the offended party or those who may have witnessed the misbehavior. Delayed intervention also takes place if another officer takes responsibility for the poor behavior and contacts the offended parties. He should then let his brother or sister officer know what he's done, and why. It is best if the offending officer rights the wrong. However any officer who has the ethical courage and the professional foresight to step in and intervene is doing the hard right over the easy wrong while likewise protecting the credibility of all involved.

Delayed intervention lets the citizen know that someone in uniform saw or heard what took place and does not condone poor behavior regardless of the circumstance. It also reminds all officers that even as we are being looked at by those not necessarily friendly to us at the moment, those who have our best personal and professional interests at heart are monitoring our actions and behavior. Better to be helped and told by a friend than confronted by a written complaint a week later!

And, further, Delayed Intervention involves the **department** itself. A good department will immediately and firmly address ethical wrongs, first by seeing to it that such violations are indeed punished swiftly and appropriately, and second, by instituting additional training for its offending officers. Such training would address the wrongs committed and show better ways to have responded. Every officer needs to know his or her department takes ethical action seriously and will act to right wrongs committed.

## Advanced Intervention

Advanced intervention is the most powerful, and therefore impactful, form of intervention available in a law enforcement organization. It is the modeling of the veteran officer who posses-ses an established reputation of ethical conduct and the practice of the first two forms of intervention noted. Such an officer is **known** throughout the department to be intolerant of misbehavior or criminal actions on the part of peace officers, regardless of their department or rank. Such an officer exudes an **Ethical Presence** that successfully stops other officers from possibly engaging in unethical conduct regardless of the circumstances or heat of the moment. Officers understand clearly that if this one officer is at a scene, or even working the street at the time, police business will be handled both ethically and lawfully. It is this impressive form of leadership **power** that the great officer strives to develop from the beginning of his or her career at the academy. Advanced intervention is simply leading by example regardless of distance or circumstance.

Departments who value such intervention, and any department worth its salt should do so, values and encourages the caliber of behavior such an officer displays. All too often, however, officers who can invoke this kind of respect are looked upon with suspicion and disdain by both management and the rank and file. The policeman's *code of silence* remains the most powerful cancer in U.S. law enforcement today, and it only remains so because leadership at the highest levels allows it to flourish.

Effective managers and supervisors cannot only exhibit ethical beliefs and behavior, they must possess the proper **value system** that keeps them focused on the job at hand and that radiates from them to correctly influence the actions and growth of those they supervise. At this moment in time, police work as a profession gives every appearance of possessing no core value system. This causes those entering the profession to become confounded by numerous, often-conflicting philosophies of behavior and action. According to some, cops must "kick ass and take names." Others say cops "must be nice to everyone and sensitive to the nuances of all cultures and upbringings." Still others say we must do both, simultaneously, and extremely well.

The law tells cops they must treat everyone equally regardless. Senior law enforcement managers put their own spin on *all of the above* and then expect their subordinate supervisors to send the right message to the street officers actually charged with doing the job. In the end what we have is the Continuity of Confusion, where only the solid ethical beliefs and value system of the individual officer can (and does on a daily basis) maintain the worth of our legal system and the society it is meant to serve and preserve.

This is the primary reason I developed the living communication art of **Verbal Judo**, which is the learned skill of verbally communicating with people skillfully and respectfully under difficult, even potentially violent circumstances. To be a consistent Verbal Judo practitioner or operator as we now call our students and instructors, we need to develop and strengthen a core **Belief** system in what and who we are. Peace officers need— and **deserve**—a better **Philosophy of Action** to adhere to during their tough daily tours of duty.

We had been exploring a solid core belief system for years in conjunction with my work with both Verbal Judo and law enforcement. I found it in the most unexpected of places—a blue-collar bar in New York City, not far from the NYPD Academy where I was teaching Verbal Judo to 400 officers each day. I had met, through an acquaintance, Mr. Jack Hoban, a former Marine captain and martial arts instructor in Ninjitsu. Mr. Hoban was, at the time, a sixth degree black belt under Grandmaster Hatsumi of Japan. I had heard of Jack for years, and had the good fortune to meet him in NY. He came to one of my Verbal Judo sessions, and later that evening, we adjourned to the aforementioned tavern.

As the tavern filled up with raucous, noisy people, I began to get irritated. I wanted to hear what Jack was saying and the noise level just continued to grow. It was distracting to me. Several times violence seemed about to break out as the alcohol flowed and people got in each other's faces. I sat there thinking all those typical negative thoughts one can under such circumstances. On the other hand, Jack quietly sat across from me with his back to a wall. All he did was talk calmly about his martial art and his students. Nothing about our environment seemed to disturb him in the least.

Finally we left. As we were walking down the street to the nearest subway station I turned to Jack. "What a bunch of jerks! What scummy people!" There was that dangerous weapon we all have, the tongue, going off again. Jack's response stunned me.

"Well, George," he said, "**at least they were safer because of our presence!**"

WHAAAAT? I'd never even considered his view of the situation. He floored me without delivering a kick or punch. I was truly humiliated. I had finally met someone who understood the **Warrior's Creed** and I had been found wanting! Throughout history, warriors have always been protectors, protectors of the weak, the innocent, and yes, even the guilty. In that increasingly turbulent tavern, not once had I had a "protector thought." Even as a police officer and tactical communications instructor all my thoughts and energy had been negative. I had allowed myself to think and act internally like the problem I was seeing and hearing. I set aside my inner calm. I thought more about me and what I wanted (to talk with and listen to Jack) than those others around me.

Jack, on the other hand, was in tune with himself. He kept his calm. He kept his awareness and readiness in both check and balance. He saw himself, and me, as the only probable protectors in the bar should someone have gotten clearly out of hand and endangered those around them. With his one simple statement to me on the way to the subway he defined the peace officer's basic core belief system.

## People Should Indeed Be Safer Because of Our Presence!

Jack's understanding of this simple belief answered my question on the subject. I asked him how he had come to frame his job, and therefore the jobs of those he supervised and influenced on a daily basis, in such a manner. He referred me to Professor Robert L. Humphrey's marvelous book, *Values for a New Millennium* (Life values press/WIN publications, 1992). Jack told me he and Professor Humphrey had been friends for years and his book had become a provocative proponent of how leaders must think, act, and behave in our growing world of respected diversity. I later read the book and was stunned by its content. Professor Humphrey defined and clarified how we can treat people equally under all circumstances, even though they may be far different than we.

The following is an excellent example of what I learned from Jack and Professor Humphrey. Professor Humphrey and some army soldiers were out hunting wild boar in a clearly Third World country. Listen to what he says:

> *As usual, on this trip, the sight of the ragged, destitute villagers drew comments from one or another American. A*

*young airman proclaimed: "Look at them; they are like a bunch of animals. What have they got to live for? They might just as well be dead." I sat in chagrined silence, but this day, in response to those familiar words, the old sergeant drawled out his answer between spits of tobacco juice. He said, "You better believe they got something to live for, Jack. If you doubt it, let me see you jump down there and try to kill one of them with your hunting knife. They'll fight you like no one ever heard of. I have fought beside them in heavy combat and I don't know either, why they seem to value their lives so much. Maybe it's them women in them pantaloons, or maybe it's them dirty faced kids; whatever it is they seem to value their lives as much as we do ours, even with all of our money. In fact, both in combat and in freezing prison camps, they hung in there after a lot of Americans were yelling quit."* (p.68)

The sergeant in this account stepped in and began conducting an immediate intervention. He pointed out "equality of life" to not only the errant and ignorant airman in question, but to those others traveling with them. He did not yell, swear, or put the airman down. He used solid communications skills based on his years of training and experience as a combat proven veteran to correct and then educate his men, as well as his commanding officer. In his book Professor Humphrey commented this clear and true approach to an unacceptable belief and hence behavior hit home with him in a way nothing had before. He asked the sergeant how he could **prove** a belief in equality despite the striking differences in wealth and advantages between the soldiers and the people they were discussing. The sergeant answered him:

*You got to be able to jump down off the truck into the sheep manure, go over there into that village of mud huts, walk down those narrow streets, and pick the dirtiest, stinkin'est village peasant that you meet; and as you walk past him, you got to be able to make him know, just with your eyes, that **you** know that he is a man who hurts like we do, and hopes like we do, and wants for his kids just like we **all** do. That's how you got to be able to do it. Nothin' else ain't going to work.* (p.69)

God love the chief or sheriff who hires men and women like this sergeant for his department and community! Despite all the measurable differences between people today there is one common connection we all share: **"We are equal in the most basic and profound respect: My life and the lives of my loved ones are as important to me as yours are to you."**

This, then, is the core belief system we should inculcate into our peace officers around the country. They are first and foremost protectors. Secondly, they understand and exhibit the belief that all people are equal on the basis of how they value their lives and the lives of their loved ones. Hence, the peace officer's treatment of those he comes into contact with, both inside and out of the department, must reflect this basic tenet of respect and exhibit the accompanying talents and skills that must go along with it for cops to properly do their jobs.

Many are the times you and I have wrestled with this challenge when in houses or places where there seemed no redeeming value, human or otherwise. Rats, dirt, bugs, filthy kids and nasty people invade our senses and trouble us to the point of anger and hostility, as well as disdain and arrogance. This is the "natural man" response. And in Verbal Judo we know that if it's natural it's probably wrong if expressed verbally. Make a note! Peace officers exist to protect all people and their right to live from those that would do them harm. Those in management, supervisory, and leadership positions must understand this basic belief system and adhere to it themselves (Talk the talk, Walk the walk), as they teach and grow such thinking among their subordinates and peers.

If this were done across the nation can you imagine how police complaints and lawsuits would drop? Can you imagine how fewer "know-it-alls" would pop up on the talk shows putting down the police? Can you imagine how much happier, more effective, and more excited your officers would be as they came to work every day knowing all they were expected to do is recognize the basic foundation of equality between all men and women...and then go about using their education, skills, and tools to *protect* and *serve* the people they are responsible for?

To become an effective and inspiring leader *you* must be able to model and then teach those around you how to relate to people and events in a manner that appears revolutionary but is in fact ancient in its source and validity. Consider how many young officers begin to think and speak after only a few months on the job. From recorded radio traffic in Los Angeles and elsewhere we *know* how the conventional police system has infected their original thought processes and belief systems. They speak of war zones and jungles. I have heard some officers quoted as saying, "This whole area could be burned to the ground and we would lose nothing." Our cops, our *peace* officers are rapidly becoming trained by their departments to see themselves not as protectors but as soldiers in Third World neighborhoods whose mission it is to simply survive their shifts and the rest of the world be damned.

We can put all the Community Policing programs we want in place and they will have no positive effect whatsoever if the officers expected to interact with the people living in their assigned neighborhoods denigrate the residents daily. A department's goal should be to bring about the belief system within its ranks that we are all one community, period. There is no such thing as a "community-policing officer"! We are *all* officers in the community and policing is our job and profession! You chiefs! Stop telling your city and county councils lies! Stop telling your men and women in uniform lies! Instead, stand up and be the leaders you were hired to be and lead your communities back into the light of day by creating within your departments a simple, teachable, understandable belief system as to what peace officers are supposed to be and why!

Indeed, the word **Supervision** becomes more understandable if we view it as meaning "Super-Sight." Effective supervisors and leaders must possess the correct Vision of right and wrong, of value and ethics for peace officers. They must model such behavior daily, everywhere, and in front of everyone to include other officers. They must actively teach and inculcate these values into the moral and mental fiber of those officers over whom they have professional control and responsibility. Leaders have the solemn duty to "Talk the Talk" and follow that talk with supervisory insistence and daily behavior that support their positions. Such a leader attains Advanced Interventional power. Moreover, in this way, a team is created, held together by a common perspective of righteous action. The great leader draws great people to him because he exudes a powerful presence and belief. One others can share in and perpetuate, and one that enriches every member of the team.

This, then, is "the good news." Peace Officers are charged with bringing peace to a turbulent and increasingly violent world. They are expected by those who pay them and those they have contact with to bring order out of disorder. As supervisors of men and women who risk their lives daily, police managers and supervisors have an obligation to actively lead by example, by work, word and deed. They must see to it that they speak and act according to what the profession represents, the protection of all the people on an equal basis and at all times under all circumstances. Effective leaders must teach and then insist on right behavior for the right reasons, and then show their officers how to properly intervene when right behavior is in jeopardy. In this way, we will put people into the field who will contact others in a manner that will generate voluntary cooperation and professional respect. In turn this leadership will enhance and enrich the professional lives of every officer such a leader touches.

## CHAPTER THREE

# THE SUPERVISOR AS CONTACT PROFESSIONAL

J ust as "Quality Contact" is the cement of quality policing, so too, is it the most necessary skill for you if you wish to lead others. So much of what we have found to be hurtful in police work results from its supervisors being **out of contact** with their officers. To be sure, working conditions, salary and benefits, and workload affect morale, but nothing affects morale more insidiously and deeply than poor communication among the officers and the Chain of Command. Officers must first **trust** their leaders. They must have **faith** that these people will do the right thing by them. And they must **believe** they are indeed whom they present themselves to be. In short, supervisors must be **credible** if they are to be leaders.

Credible supervisors and leaders are **in contact** first with themselves. They know who they are and what they represent. They are ethical and they perpetuate the appropriate value system that others are encouraged to believe in and share. In the last chapter, we looked carefully at the substance of both of these issues. In this chapter, we will examine what the successful leader needs to **know** about the Profession of Law Enforcement in order to generate confidence in his or her people.

In the basic Verbal Judo class we teach that the goal of law enforcement is to bring Order out of Disorder and to **generate voluntary compliance**. Officers must talk and act in such a way as to motivate people to do what they must do, according to law, whether they agree with the process or not. Officers are safer when they are capable of generating voluntary compliance, as are the people they serve. Interestingly enough, Leadership has the same goal—**to generate voluntary compliance!** You might also think of it as generating voluntary commitment and/or collaboration, depending on the circumstances. Supervisors and leaders must talk and act in such a way as to encourage their subordinates to do what needs to be done, especially in their absence! Indeed, we believe the real test of effective supervision is the supervisor's absence. If officers perform correctly, as they are required to when their supervisor is absent, we can deduce they believe in both themselves and in their leadership and choose to demonstrate positive performance voluntarily. Weak or mistrusted supervisors constantly look over the shoulders of their people and strive daily to convince them that their presence is necessary for effective behavior. Minimal performance supervisors fear to delegate their authority as to do so might reveal how ineffective, unknowing, and unnecessary their presence in management truly is. They exalt ruling with an "iron hand" because they themselves are suspect. This is primarily because, despite an outward successful appearance, the weak leader lacks what it takes to develop and then oversee a healthy subordinate. Weak supervisors, who almost always become the proverbial office bully, use rules, regulations, and a flurry of paperwork to hammer their subordinates into involuntary compliance. They micro-manage people and performance to death. The results of such negative leadership cripples the effectiveness of their department over time and tears away at the quality of service provided to the community as a whole.

Verbal Judo leaders understand that the two most effective Force Options they can use to generate voluntary compliance among their subordinates are **Presence** and **Words**. We talked about Presence in the last chapter. It is the force exuded by the ethical and healthy supervisor as he interacts with his people. His just "being there" is a crucial part of Advanced Intervention, the most important aspect of resolving issues before they become serious problems. But the power of presence is seen in many smaller things, such as how the supervisor wears his uniform, how he walks, and how he handles his newfound responsibilities and authority. And perhaps most significant to Presence is his Professional Face, how he looks at his officers when he addresses them either individually or collectively, and how he looks to his subordinates as he interacts with them.

The *right* look is worth a thousand words. Whenever your face is not consistent or consonant with what you are saying people will believe the face and not the words coming out of its mouth. Far too many supervisors betray their negative personal feelings, and perhaps their *real* feelings, in their expressions even while they believe they are fooling their audience with sugar-coated, politically correct language. When this happens they instantly lose credibility with the people they are dealing with. How often have we seen people say they are interested, yet they clearly look uninterested? Or, they say they care but clearly look as if they could care less? All too often!

An officer we know once approached a weak supervisor in his chain of command and challenged the content of a behind-the-scenes conversation between the patrol captain and the sergeant in question. Appearing to listen to the officer the sergeant kept glancing away, and fussing with a non-compliant copier machine. When the officer, in exasperation, asked the sergeant if he were listening the supervisor replied, "Yes, of course I am. Go on." The officer paused a moment, then turned and went to the patrol captain's office where he announced in no uncertain terms if the sergeant wasn't interested enough to discuss the situation and perhaps resolve it in a positive manner, the officer would consider filing a union complaint against him. This because to the officer, based on the sergeant's betraying Professional Face, he had indeed probably slandered the officer to the patrol captain.

If you are a struggling supervisor, it may be because you have not yet learned this essential leadership skill: **the ability to adapt to those subordinates you supervise!** The effective supervisor must be a **Chameleon!** Chameleons survive and THRIVE successfully because they can change their appearance in a **credible** manner as conditions and people change around them; they blend and harmonize with their environment. Do not confuse this adaptive skill with willful deception or dishonesty. True, such flexibility and plasticity could be used for negative ends. But as we mean it here the ability to adapt is the foundation of anyone who deals with people different from himself or people one may not personally like or agree with. The great supervisor **becomes** who he has to be to handle the situation at hand. And he does so to achieve the higher and greater goal for both his subordinates and his organization.

It is not possible to like everyone we work with or for; it is not possible to respect everyone we work with or meet in the street, but it is necessary to handle them in such a way as to generate their voluntary compliance whenever possible. We cannot do this if we supervise from the basis of our personal feelings. Indeed, not one of us is hired as a peace officer to do our job based upon personal feelings. We believe the moment you let natural words, or words coming "from the heart," leave your lips you will usually say things you will regret almost immediately if not sooner. Peace officers are hired to get their job done as effectively and efficiently as possible, and so they must **say** what is necessary and proper while at the same time **presenting** the right face. A face consonant with the words and tone of voice they are using at the time. The truly successful supervisor and leader possess a hundred faces, a thousand different voices, when working with his officers. Make a note! The appropriate face and voice are the effective leader's stage props when it comes to creative and successful supervision.

**Words** are Force Option Two. We break this Option down into three sections for the successful supervisor. Unless we are under emergency conditions, where we order and demand instant compliance, Level One is to **ask** for cooperation.

It seems so simple, doesn't it? Yet too many supervisors have forgotten or lost this elemental verbal communications skill, if they ever had it! Too many supervisors today habitually **tell** people what to do. Like their subordinates they forget or perhaps choose not to ask first; it is easier to demand than to request. Make a note! People like to be asked; doing so is a sign of respect and, in more cases than not, the respectful and polite request will be honored. For some supervisors, especially those who possess Type-A personalities, *relearning* to ask is difficult. However, the results will more than exceed the pain of self-appraisal and personal behavior modification. You will literally see it occur before your very eyes even as the words "Could you please..." leave your mouth!

Sometimes simply asking an employee or subordinate to do something is not enough. Perhaps the task is a complicated one, or the action or activity goes against what the individual is used to doing or believes should be done. In this instance the astute supervisor moves to Level Two of the verbalization process and that is the **Art of Persuasion**. Here is where you use the Verbal Judo patented **Five-Step Hard Style** matrix. If you have not been through the basic Verbal Judo class, the following will be unfamiliar territory. Allow us to briefly define the matrix to help you along at this point. The police supervisor maintains far better **contact** and hence power with his people if he is persuasive rather than autocratic.

Step 1 in our matrix is **Ask**, at least twice, that the subordinate voluntarily comply. Step 2, **Set the Context**. Here you answer the perhaps unspoken question why. Why the request is being made, and the conditions under which the request is necessary. When you tell people why you accomplish a number of powerful things. One, you set your professional ground, whether it be the law, the regulations, or the policies that must be followed. You use the Rational Appeal of reason and logic to show that your request makes good sense and is in line with departmental needs. Two, by so describing the reasons for your request, you establish a "professional face" with your audience and eliminate the "personal face" issues that the other person may have heard or imagined in your initial request. And, perhaps most importantly, by simply explaining to people why something needs to be done you show respect for them. People have a natural tendency to want to know why, indeed, many feel they have a constitutional right to know why, and when you tell them they more often than not will cooperate. Our research shows that a minimum of seven out of ten people will do what you want them to if you will only tell them why it must be done! This is a powerful statistic. And these are people who are outside of your organization. Imagine the greater efficiency, lessened stress, and better work environment you as a leader and supervisor can create by informing in a constructive manner those who work for you! Knowingly, or unknowingly, subordinates will feel fairly treated if you demonstrate you have respect for their personage and their professional status. Unfortunately in the law enforcement work environment far too many supervisors talk to and treat their officers **worse** than the way they treat suspects or the average citizen. Why? Because they believe they **can**! And because the organization may allow them to "do" because they "can," this category of supervisor generates issues and problems for all those around him.

Should Step 2 not achieve the desired result (voluntary compliance) you move to Step Three, **Options**. Here you carefully and logically lay out for your subordinate what's in it for him if he voluntarily goes along with the program. We know people are naturally responsive in a positive manner to those things that they recognize will benefit them. When the police supervisor engages a resistive officer, or the office manager a resistive employee, he seeks to use personal appeal as a means to gain understanding and then voluntary compliance. Personal Appeal relies on the principle that people will do what you want them to do if you can show that what you want them to do is **good for them**. Notice the word **show**. In Step 2 we tell; in Step 3 we show. You describe as specifically as possible what the advantages are to the person when he or she acts in accordance with your requests. You give the best options first. Then you offer the not-so-good options. Most peace officers do this in reverse and then wonder why they are still debating with the subject once it's all said and done. Give the best options first and see what the difference is! Giving negative options or results up front creates confrontation and anger, and confrontation and anger close down communication channels fast. Let the resistive subordinate know how he'll benefit right up front and that's what he'll focus on even as he's hearing the downside of not going along with you voluntarily at the tail end of your conversation.

Creating and presenting options to resistant people is a cop's job. Peace officers present options on a daily basis to redirect angry and hostile people and persuade them to move in more positive directions. Good supervisors must do the same with their employees...and when they do they teach their employees how to mirror such behavior with those they, in turn, come into contact with. This, then, is good mentorship, and good leadership.

There are **three secrets** to presenting options successfully. **First secret**, when you present your option or options, make your **voice** friendly and helpful, even if the other was rude and insulting! To make your voice such, even when you do not feel such, is the essence of **tactical communication**! The other must believe you care that he does the right thing. If your voice is negative, he will resist and fight you. If you make your voice pleasant and befitting the options offered, he has no one to fight and he can actually save personal face and accept the better options. The good supervisor must 'chameleon up', must become who he has to be to be successful at step 3 or it will not work.

**Secret two, be specific!** Encourage the person by your words and facial expression/body language to recognize the distinct positive advantages to him if he takes advantage of the best options. Paint a specific picture of the positives and the negatives, **always** giving the positive first. Specifics sober people up, they make people **see**! You cannot do this, of course, if you do not know your people. You must be "in contact" with your people so you know what they value and what they could care less about. The Verbal Judo supervisor is specific because what might be of significance to one party could be absolutely irrelevant to another. One great weakness of some supervisors is that they think they must (and do) treat everyone "the same way." They have been lied to and convinced to believe such treatment is fair. Equitable treatment is not the same as persuading your employees or subordinates, all of whom are unique individuals in their own right, to undertake those things you wish or need them to voluntarily. This is fair treatment at its best. Seeing and working with others as individuals and not as a block of numbers is the ultimate in fair and equal treatment.

Treating everyone the same is lazy leadership and the mark of an uncreative and uncaring supervisor. The Verbal Judo supervisor wants to get to know his or her employees or subordinates individually: what they value and why. Only in this way can a supervisor's options possess the kind of positive power that moves someone opposite you from one position to another in voluntary compliance and for the Good of the Order.

We have already touched on the **third secret**. It is **Always Present the Positive Option(s) First!** Failure to follow this rule will lead to disaster! Again, it is **tactical**, not "natural" to put the positive first when we offer options or alternatives. In our society we've been taught over the years to "lower the boom" right away. Tell 'em what's gonna happen to them if they don't do this or do that. Make 'em squirm and then send them back to work! This approach is fraught with down sides, but, it is so easy to do when you as a supervisor are irritated or frustrated with a subordinate.

It is all too easy to put the negative first: "If you do not follow my orders, you will suffer the consequences." When people hear this they immediately shut down, then fail to recognize whatever "carrot" you try to offer after you've pissed them off. When we put the negative first it becomes a threat and creates what we call threat resistance. Once threat resistance rears its very powerful head you as a supervisor have now created enormous hurdles to overcome. Anything said can and will be used against you later, either behind your back or with union representatives or attorneys.

It is a **tactical** move in communications to offer the positive first because it works, as we've described, more often than not. When we corner people they will fight for their survival, whether physical, mental, or emotional. When we leave them with a safe and respectful way out, a way where they recognize they will benefit, they will most often take it. When the Verbal Judo supervisor combines Secrets 1, 2 and 3, he creates a persuasion formula nearly irresistible! Our studies and experience have shown us that a minimum of nine out of ten people will willfully choose to comply if approached in this manner. Try it. We believe you'll find the results amazing.

What about the hardcore employee? The one who continues to resist and elects not to comply? The Verbal Judo supervisor then moves to Step 4, **Confirmation**. We want to **confirm** that the resistance we are encountering is real and liable to continue. Verbally the rebellious employee is provided one final opportunity rather than "one last chance." We say, **"Is there anything I can say at this point to gain your voluntary compliance in this matter? I'd like to think there is."** At this point, you, as a supervisor, have put the ball back in the errant employee's court. It has now become his final decision in the process. He can save "face" by choosing to comply and everyone can move on. You as a leader and supervisor have not threatened him or backed him into a corner, and he can't later claim you didn't allow or provide him every opportunity to work with you on his problem or challenge. As in Step 3, the secret here is to voice this confirmatory sentence as pleasantly as you can. Sell voluntary compliance! Match the face with the message and the tone in which it is presented.

No one reading this book likes to feel or be threatened. The Verbal Judo supervisor understands this and goes the extra mile to ensure the employee cannot claim anything other than appropriate and constructive direction was always in the offering and available through voluntary compliance. Give your employee the opportunity to rise to the occasion. When he or she does, grab onto the offered hand and hold it tight! You've now won an important battle in your professional relationship. From this point on the employee is working with, not against you.

At the opposite end of the scale you must listen carefully for **equal or increasing resistance** coming from the employee. We teach officers on the street, handling potentially violent or resistant subjects, that the moment they hear equal or more resistance from the subject, they are to **Act**, which is Step 5 in the Hard Style matrix. For supervisors facing involuntary compliance, which is where you are when the employee or subject fails to respond to the positive options offered, direct action is now the only remedy left. At this point the Verbal Judo supervisor will issue an **order** to the subject to comply with the original request, recommendation, or suggestion. In more cases than not most rebellious employees will comply for whatever reason in their minds is logical.

What if they do not? The Force Options for supervisors are not like those of the street officer dealing with a combative drunk. In the administrative world there is the written warning, followed by time off (with or without pay), disciplinary transfer, or eventually voluntary resignation or involuntary termination. What is crucial for you, the Verbal Judo supervisor, is to *know and understand the system* you are working within. Know what you can do at your level and what you can't. Nothing will lose you credibility quicker than threatening to do something that you cannot do at your level! Nothing will lead to a lawsuit quicker than jumping appropriate levels of discipline and not following due process. You must study the system, know the book, chapter and verse, so you will not make misstatements or take inappropriate actions. The Contact Professional and Verbal Judo supervisor knows his organization backwards and forwards and he knows the "fine print" in the Rules and Regulations. Knowledge is truly power and true knowledge used wisely is power-FUL! Lackluster supervisors cut corners and bully their employees into some form of obedience. This works only until they encounter the one employee who knows more than they do and is not afraid to *take them out* using the very policies and procedures the supervisor is expected to be guided and bound by.

For example, one morning a new supervisor strolled into the office he shared with another supervisor in the organization. He immediately noticed his office mate was not wearing the normal work attire expected of everyone else when they arrived for work. Taking his peer to task he pointed out the violation and spent considerable time "dressing down" the other man, ensuring that he touched upon how the rest of the office would react if the leadership didn't follow the rules for office dress. When he had finished, the subject of this sanctimonious tirade quietly pointed out that he, the accuser, was likewise "out of uniform." And indeed the tormenter was. What followed was a pointless argument about who was right and who was wrong, which was unfortunately overheard by more than one subordinate in the outer offices. Although the one supervisor was indeed wrong in how he came to work that morning he was able—successfully—to deflect his peer's admonition and on-the-spot correction due to an equal violation of the same rule by the party attempting to do the correcting! Verbal Judo supervisors and managers and leaders ensure they themselves are first and foremost on solid ground before they exert their authority. Otherwise their authority becomes subject to ridicule, doubt, and ultimately challenge.

The effective and dynamic leader, then, will be **in contact** with the *goal* of what we title Verbal Judo Leadership-and that is voluntary compliance. This includes the entire range of administrative and communications *force options* at the Verbal Judo leader's disposal to generate such compliance. Knowing and pursuing this goal keeps the VJ leader on track. Everything he does, he does in terms of seeking to generate voluntary compliance so the right goals, both as an organization and individual, are reached as a team. How does the VJ supervisor pursue the organization's goals as well as his own for those employees working for him?

Verbal Judo supervisors must develop a specific **Habit of Mind** called **Mushin**. This Japanese word means "no mind" or *still center*. Taught to the ancient Samurai warriors *mushin* is the ability of the warrior to be surrounded by attackers and yet remain calm and focused on the goal of gaining victory regardless of the odds arrayed against him. Instead of becoming tense or fearful, the warrior achieves a still center that allows him to respond to any attack using all his skills and training in the appropriate manner and with appropriate timing. We teach street officers this skill, and it is similarly useful to supervisors who often find themselves in a "war" of personalities and conflicting demands. Another word for *Mushin* is **disinterested**. Properly defined this is the ability to be open, flexible, and above all, **unbiased** in all interactions with people. We believe that to be immensely successful in leading, developing, and influencing people as a leader you have to be interested in their success on your behalf, but at the same time **disinterested** in how you promote this success on *their* behalf.

There are three kinds of people with whom we interact:

1. **Nice** people
2. **Difficult** people
3. **Wimps**

**Nice** people are cooperative almost by nature. They want to please and they rarely get upset about little things. They work well within systems, they value relationships with others, and they value group effort. We call these people "single key" people, meaning it only takes one key, one attempt, to obtain their voluntary compliance. Ask them and they perform. No complex tactics are needed, no unnecessary effort is expended, but it would be a mistake to think you therefore can handle such people roughly. You do not want to erode the confidence that Nice people have in the police. Remember, these people serve on juries and they vote for pay raises! Be nice!

**Difficult** people are not so easy. Difficult people ask why, they question authority naturally, and they require being convinced or persuaded. I, myself, am such a person. My co-author is, as well. When told what I should do, I naturally ask why, who says, how are you so sure, and I tend to look for a better way, often "my way" to achieve the goal required of me. People like Greg and me are called "multi-keyed" because one key never opens the door to our voluntary compliance. Difficult people in the Verbal Judo world are often the skeptics, the naysayers, the "squeaky wheel" people. Not easy to manage, they often irritate the driving, bottom line supervisor who gets impatient with their perceived resistance.

Street cops tend to be difficult people by nature. They are highly independent on the street, and they themselves supervise hundreds and even thousands of people on a daily basis, so they are oft seen as challenging to lead or manage. And yet, often such officers have the best ideas about what ought to be done, but their supervisors have a hard time with their suggestions because the suggestions are often presented in the challenging, hard-core manner that irritates those in charge. Street officers who are difficult people tend to present their ideas forcefully and in a straightforward way, without sugar-coating or frosting! Their everyday world does not have much room for office politics or butt kissing.

The successful leader and supervisor needs to learn to value these "difficult" people! Learn to love the rough presenters (and often characters) because, if you listen to them, you will often learn what you need to know: what is working and what is not! They will rarely tell you what you want to hear, but they will tell you the truth, as they see and experience it. Successful leaders deal with such people **tactically**, using the best listening skills and relying on persuasion rather than fiat. Our experience has shown us that if you use the Five Steps with difficult people, nine out of ten will cooperate with you by Step 3, Options. They value being told why and they value being given an opportunity to make their own decisions. Orders, commands, and brusque treatment make these people instantly resistant, and over time, they can become enemies that can and will hurt your career and make your daily supervisory life miserable!

We recall the story of the sergeant who, in dealing with an officer considered difficult, elected to describe the corrective action he wanted to effect as actually coming from one of the local deputy district attorneys. The officer, who routinely met with the different lawyers in the DA's Office, became immediately suspect and at the end of the formal counseling session he called the Deputy DA in question and related what had been attributed to him by the sergeant. The DDA confirmed the sergeant did indeed contact him for an opinion on the law and procedure in question but that what the sergeant attributed to him was not what he'd told the officer's supervisor. With this information in hand the officer then obtained the correct and accurate information now being provided by a perhaps vengeful DDA. He then wrote the information up in a formal memo with a copy to the department's chief, stating quite diplomatically how the sergeant was in error and what was actually correct and proper on the subject...per the DDA. From this point on the sergeant was never able to effectively manage this officer, and the department's chief now had questions about his sergeant's understanding of the law and proper procedure as dictated by the DA's office.

With Difficult people, you, the Verbal Judo supervisor, have to make a significant change from the norm. We know from research in effective communication, that approximately 93% of your effectiveness lies in your *Delivery Style*, your voice and other non-verbals. Only 7-10% of your effectiveness lies in your *Content*, or message. You must pay attention to these figures when you communicate, for if your delivery is poor, your impact will be poor. **But**, do not count on your officers or employees knowing the same things you now do; do not count on them caring; and do not count on them having taken a Verbal Judo course that taught them the importance of delivery. **You**, as a supervisor, must ignore their delivery and concentrate on the substance of their remarks. You must tactically ignore their attitudes in favor of their meanings. **"Let their attitude drift, focus only on the meanings."** You must stay **in contact** with them despite their communication shortcomings.

It is natural to feel irritation, even dislike, upon hearing a perhaps rough presentation, but such a response on a leader or supervisor's part is not effective. When you let irritation rule, you no longer listen, and you shut down, failing to perceive the potential value of the discourse. Over time, if you can maintain disinterest as we define the concept, remain open and unbiased, such people will gradually become easier for you to deal with for they will learn you can and do listen, regardless of how they deliver their message to you. They will grow to trust you not to take things personally, and their professional estimate of you will rise considerably with this growing perception and understanding.

**Sneaky people** are a real problem no matter how you cut it. By definition, they are highly problematic people, showing you one thing but thinking another, saying one thing but meaning another. They are the *"Oh, Yes"* people to your face, but the *"Oh, No!"* people behind your back.

A large number of **sneaky people** are **wimps**, fearful of conflict or honesty. They will say whatever they think you want to hear, out of fear or for some self-serving purpose. They are not "up front" people; they are two-faced. One face they show, the other they keep hidden. If they do not like you, they will undermine you behind your back and at every opportunity. They sound like *nice* people, but that is the beauty of their illusion. If you have power in an organization, these people will always cater to you, they will always agree with you, and they will never take issue with you, but they are not your friends, much less your supporters! The supervisor who gathers WIMPS to his side, as many do, cuts himself off from the truth and has no real lasting strength.

It may be difficult to identify such *wimps*, at least initially. The Verbal Judo supervisor will therefore treat everyone with equal tactical politeness and caution. As time passes, you will learn who the wimps are, either from backroom hearsay or by seeing, hearing, and experiencing how their actions conflict with their words. Once identified, you simply accept them for what they are, and cease being surprised by their duplicity.

You can also establish a "trusting relationship" with them that makes them feel they can trust you more than the average person and hence blunt their tendency to say one thing and do another when dealing with you. Wimps, however, are poison to an organization unless properly and swiftly identified by their immediate supervisor and then brought to bay using sound managerial and disciplinary techniques. Wimps can and do destroy good subordinates and employees for their own purposes, and likewise will take down a good supervisor or manager for the same twisted personal agendas. *Wimps* are seldom converted to becoming *Difficult* or even *Nice* people per the Verbal Judo definitions of such folks. Wimps, sadly, are and always will be Wimps. The key is to recognize them as such and effectively manage them up to and including termination.

But there is a second, more dangerous subgroup here known as **wolves in sheep's clothing**! Sneaky people may just wish to mislead you, blunt your alertness and misdirect you. I always mention in class to street officers that people they stop for infractions and who are excessive or unnaturally "nice" may in fact be wolves with hidden, dangerous agendas. Perhaps they do not wish to give the officer the opportunity to look further into their case. Perhaps they hope their "good attitude" will blind the officer and allow him to miss crucial clues.

Whatever the case, we know that it is **not natural** for people who have been stopped and who are getting a ticket or arrested to present a good attitude. People who presented such to me in the field always activated my internal alarm system. They were either 1) truly **nice people** who were truly sorry they committed an error, or 2) they were **wolves** who wished to deceive me. In an organization, such wolves undermine and undercut your efforts and your reputation to forward their own causes, and they truly should not to be taken lightly!

What should be clear at this point is that you must be **skillful** with all three kinds of people. You must be **in contact** with their unique behavioral tendencies, and therefore capable of **becoming who you must become** in order to handle each with respect and skill—the Chameleon at his best!

A large part of staying in **contact** with people is not letting them upset you or provoke you to anger. On the streets, police officers are often met by insults and name calling, and they must be able to handle such verbal attacks in a disinterested and insightful "no mind" manner. At the Verbal Judo Institute we teach them an array of "verbal deflectors" to help them successfully manage insulting people. So, too, must the supervisor be able to deflect verbal abuse, sometimes from his subordinates or employees, but more often from those above him, higher in rank.

The "natural reaction" to an insult is direct confrontation, a lashing back at the attacker, but such reaction only precipitates further escalation, possibly violence. We recommend a more studied, tactical response of deflection and redirection. As ancient Samurai wisdom puts it, "If man throw spear at head, move head. Spear miss, man now disarmed, and now it is your turn." Certain tactical phrases used at the proper moment in time can enable you to deflect anything someone says to you. If you are called an idiot by a ranking superior, for example (something we have heard occur in more than one police department) a proper verbal deflector might be, "Sorry you feel that way, but…" or "I hear that, but…" or "I can see you're upset, Sir, but…" Any one of these deflectors can accomplish several powerful things for you. One, you **feel good**, for you are armed and ready for such assaults. Two, your response is a **springboard-focus** tactic: the phrase, "I hear that," for example, springboards you quickly to the word "but" which is your focus word. Thompson's Law follows: **every word following the "but" must be tailored to the professional goal at hand!** "I hear that, Sir, but perhaps the officers' recommendations have some merit not immediately seen. For example…"

Note that you have not been drawn into a personal argument and you have stayed focused on the issue at hand. You have remained professional and in so doing have achieved a third advantage—you have **disarmed** the attacker. Failing to hit home, to upset your balance, he must now address only the issue before him. And last, fourth, in using verbal deflectors you **sound good** to all those who may be in the area, enhancing your reputation and protecting yourself at perhaps his expense.

The art of verbal deflection, the vocal art that allows you to maintain Mushin and speak professionally, rests on three underlying principles that will successfully guide you in any encounter.

**Principle One, "Say what you want, do what I say."** If street officers follow this, they literally avoid almost all citizen complaints. If you think about it people have a right to speak their minds to you, like it or not, but they must do what the officer says if his directions are lawful. Supervisors can use this same principle to avoid confrontations that result when their subordinates grumble and mutter words they may not like hearing. You do not want to make every verbal issue a matter of "insubordination." Subordinates and employees need to vent, and venting verbally hurts less than a good fistfight! Should a superior speak harshly to you during a discussion, it should not matter to you as long as he goes along with your recommendations. Your ideas should be more important to you than your ego or his bad behavior. Your superior can say what he wants as long as in the end he does what you recommend for the good of the whole. At the same time your subordinates can say what they wish as long as in the end they do what you, as their manager or supervisor, direct.

Bear this in mind. Insubordination is a serious offense in the workplace. At the same time most supervisors have no clue as to what constitutes true insubordination and in their ignorance they can open up a can of worms that they will never crawl out from under. The Verbal Judo supervisor KNOWS THE SYSTEM he is working in and understands correct definitions. Simple venting is something to be expected and can be used in your favor as a manager. Insubordination is a wholly different matter and must be dealt with well within the constraints of established policy, procedure, and rule.

**Principle Two, "I've got the last act, you've got the last word."** This principle harmonizes with Principle One, especially if you are in a leadership position. In such a role you do have the last act, you can and will do what you can and need to, so it is important to let those under your direction have the last word at times. Having the last word helps people save face and by giving them this small token of respect you create a "win-win" situation. Simply remember that in the end your rule is the final determination regardless of what is said last.

**Principle Three** is the most crucial one and must be adhered to at all times. It is **"the Golden Rule of the Street"** for police officers and translates as **"treat the other as you would want to be treated under identical conditions!"** In Verbal Judo we call this **RE**-spect with the emphasis on the **RE**. We distinguish this from the normal word respect because although we cannot "respect" everyone, we can show him or her operational RE-spect at all times. At no time is it permissible to show another human being disrespect! When people are disrespected, they all too often seek confrontation and sometimes revenge. We teach that "disrespect" is dis'em, and dis'em is death! In Latin "Dis" means "no." In street slang, "don't 'dis' me" means do not treat me like a no, or non-person. In too many work environments and families DISrespect is a way of life! In such environments, supervisors or parents disrespect their employees or family members and the disrespected respond by disrespecting those they feel below them. It's a vicious, unpardonable cycle that accomplishes only the negative.

These three principles, then, must guide our interactions and verbal encounters if we seek to stay **in contact** with our people. But it all starts with your desire to become whom you have to be to truly succeed at leading others. You just can't be "yourself." You must in some way re-create yourself, and re-creation starts with knowing yourself, your strengths and your weaknesses and then shaping and evolving these to achieve leadership qualities, traits, and successful behaviors. We all have weaknesses in dealing with people, and unless these are clearly defined and dealt with, we will always slip back into inappropriate actions and reactions, especially under stress. The great Contact Professional is always, first and foremost, in contact with himself, the "self" he or she wishes to present to others!

Remember and seek to become the Verbal Judo Chameleon!

Let us suggest a simple but effective way to handle your personal shortcomings as an evolving leader and supervisor.

There are only three steps to follow:

**Define** a shortcoming,
**Name it**, and
**YOU** will forever **Control it!**

Let us give you a personal example. One of both my co-author and my weaknesses was having our authority challenged. Someone would say, "You can't do this to me," and we would immediately seek to prove him or her **wrong**! We noticed over time that every time we received such challenges, a little voice went off in our heads that said, "Wanna bet! Watch me!" Then we would react! We realized we had to first **define** our personal and then professional shortcoming, which was: "He who challenges my authority." In my case, I chose to **name** such people as "Mister Wanna Bet." My co-author named him "Mr. You-Don't-Get-It." We began retraining our negative response to these two challengers by saying, "George/Greg, beware of 'Mister Wanna-Bet-You-Don't-Get-It'." Giving our self-imposed nemesis a name now helped us recognize the enemy. The next time we were confronted by such a person, a new voice now went off in our heads: "Here he is, 'Mister...,' be careful George/Greg!" We would now take a tactical rather than a reactive verbal stance. We had control. We knew our enemy. We overcame our natural, non-productive reaction.

The real enemies are the people who get to you for they make you **react** rather than **respond**; they make you act "naturally" rather than tactically. Defining and naming one's enemies creates new "voices" in your head that replaces the negative and perhaps explosive ones. You literally create an internal warning system that tells you when you are in danger of reacting, and being controlled by others! As a supervisor, leader, and manager, this kind of personal power is an absolute necessity.

Once you can control yourself, you are ready to become a good Representative. The great Contact Professional stands between a rock and a hard place, he stands between what he must represent, the organization and its laws, policies, and regulations, and his people. The Art of Representation requires you to represent your organization, and all it stands for, to your people, **in such a way as to generate voluntary compliance!** Think of a Figure Eight, with you in the center, the "star," the department pictured as a circle on the left and your people on the right, depicted in a box. See the illustration below.

Start in the middle, with you as speaker. As you speak, you must represent the left side (the department) to the right side (your people), in such a manner and in such a way as to bring your people into compliance with the left side. If you draw repeatedly, starting in the middle, and going left to right, left to right, over and over, then, finally draw an arrow from far right, through the center, back to the circle on the left, showing compliance achieved, you will see your figure eight clearly depicted. Notice the figure below drawn, as it should look.

This Figure Eight is what good representation looks like. Let's define the pieces of the pattern more clearly. The department is a circle, suggesting the purity of the law, policies, procedures, the city/county, the Chief, the Sheriff, or the Director and finally the U.S. Constitution and the Bill of Rights! The box on the right is a symbol of potential "brain damage" some of your people may be under. Individual desires, competing interests, and so forth. Notice that the energy field created by your representation rounds off the rough edges of the box and brings your group, your team, back into voluntary compliance (the arrow) with the organization and all it represents.

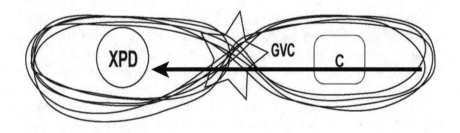

Above all, notice that the energy field of your presentation nearly obliterates you, the "star" in the middle. Only the five points of the star can now be seen. What's the point? A major one: You must disappear to have positive influence over others! The five discernable star points stand for what you are representing, and you, the personality, have disappeared. Another Thompson Law: to have power over others, you personally must disappear! Ironically, the display of Ego is your worst enemy. Your power with people goes dramatically UP as your ego goes dramatically down! The trick is to stay "centered," in the middle, effectively representing both sides in an attempt to achieve the professional goals at hand.

The Figure Eight also makes it easy to see what blunders a supervisor can make. The most obvious is ego. Think how many supervisors and administrators have huge, out of control egos!

They have come to believe their own press! They gather and rely on those who feed their egos and growing sense of "I'm always right...even if I'm wrong!" Subordinates and those others affected by such supervisors and their egos learn to hate these people, always professionally and sometimes personally. When this occurs, ego-driven (riddled?) administrators, managers, and supervisors have no real influence over others possessing a healthy positive nature. Puffed up by their own self-generated importance, they only serve themselves and no one or thing else. They become disloyal. They seek to destroy all those who do not feed their egos. They create nightmare work environments to be suffered and endured by those under them.

They often articulate either in public or private that poor morale in their organization is not their fault.

An example of this is when a weak sergeant goes before his troops at roll call and says, "This policy is really crap, but we have to go along with it, so make it work somehow." It might not be the policy; it might be the Chief, or the Commander, or the Lieutenant, but whoever or whatever it is the sergeant makes it clear he thinks it is (or they are) crap. He undermines it (or them) verbally to make himself look better to his troops and to place the blame for doing something elsewhere. If you, the supervisor, do not like something, you properly take it up with your peers and superiors and fight the case from there. Once legislated, however, as the department's representative, you are subordinated to carry the word to the troops and make it both stick and work. Should your troops complain, tell them to gather as much evidence as they can from the field to prove the policy is not working well and how it might be improved and give it to you. You then can go back to the command levels and make a responsible case for a second look at the policy. Never undermine, by word or deed, that which you are expected to represent. Only cowards do this! Moreover, though your troops might "like" you for agreeing with them, they will never respect you. They know cowardice when they see or hear it!

Another fatal mistake for you, the supervisor, is to undermine your troops to curry favor with your superiors. When the troops complain that something is not working on the street and you fail to check it out you are undermining those under you. How? Because you fear the repercussions, the flack, the fallout that you anticipate from delivering bad news above their level. As we pointed out earlier weak supervisors always "sugar-coat" negative feedback from their troops to save their own butts! The good supervisor will represent his men and women to the Command level in such a way as to encourage them to respond to the concerns of the street officers for the betterment of the organization. Too often troops feel the Brass is "unresponsive" to their needs. Employees' needs and observations must be conveyed to the Brass by their front-line supervisors. If the front-line supervisor fails to take the message forward, everyone suffers. The troops never get a real hearing, and the Command people never hear the complete, unalloyed message.

The Contact Professional never betrays his men and women. He puts their concerns and needs ahead of his own by representing them clearly and courageously. Thompson's Law: **"Look down to your people and ye shall rise up."** Rather than looking upward, currying favor and jockeying for a better rank, the supervisor with integrity looks down to (not at) his people, assesses their needs, and brings these forward with courage. As the supervisor makes a meaningful impression on the Command staff, and gets them to respond appropriately to the problems articulated, the problems on the street decrease and the troops work with greater effectiveness and better morale. Their activity improves, the good "stats" increase, and the team begins to get noticed from above. As they get noticed, you get noticed, and your own career will only be enhanced!

Indeed, the Contact Professional is the ultimate supervisor. He possesses "super-sight" because he listens and responds to his people. He exudes ethics and a solid, clearly defined value system, and he believes, above all, that he is there for his troops.

The great supervisors we have worked with and witnessed over time taught us the following Law: **"The moment you get promoted, the moment you get your stripes, your bars, your stars, you will never again do a single solitary thing to advance your career because your personal career is now meaningless. What is meaningful is the careers and welfare of your people!"**

A great teacher once said that his entire goal in teaching was to get his students to go beyond him, to exceed his level of accomplishment and competence. The great leader, supervisor, or manager cultivates his people and makes his assignments and personnel decisions in an effort to get the best from each individual. Rather than promote himself, he promotes his people.

Much of a supervisor's stress will disappear if he comes to work each day with one objective in mind-take care of his people! As your people advance, you advance. It's truly the only Way!

## CHAPTER FOUR

# THREE SURVIVAL TRUTHS FOR QUALITY COMMUNICATION

L et us recommend the three following Street Truths of quality communication that will make you smarter about dealing with people and handling yourself and your image within a police department or other organization. Most people do not know these, and I learned them when I moved from college teaching into police work. I often preach these in my Verbal Judo classes, but I have only written about one of them in my previous books. Study carefully the following Street Truths for they make all the difference between success and failure as a leader and manager of others.

## 1. PEOPLE NEVER SAY WHAT THEY MEAN!

If this first survival truth startles you, be assured learning this startled us, too!

No college or academy course ever teaches what you learn on the streets as an officer about language. Because I, for example, was constantly answering calls where people were upset, it finally dawned on me that what I was hearing was not what was truly meant as uttered. What finally woke me up was a particular burglary call where, when I arrived, the man at the door screamed at me about being late answering the call: "I called hours ago, you incompetent S-O-B!" He ranted and raved for several minutes about the department and me in particular. I listened to his words of rage, anger, and frustration and I felt my own anger begin to build. After all, I had been very busy on my last call trying to mediate a domestic dispute and had arrived just as soon as possible. I felt like lashing back, telling him how wrong he was and if he didn't like our service, he could handle the call himself! At the same time, I felt some empathy. I, too, had once been the victim of a break-in and I remembered my own feelings. It suddenly struck me that the man in front of me really meant **Help me**, dammit! Indeed, as I thought through it, I saw behind the words to the five levels of meaning he was trying to express.

1. I need help!
2. What about my stuff?
3. I feel fearful, life's not the way I thought it was, safe and secure;
4. I feel raped, violated! And,
5. Time—where have you been?

Yes, the first four were really what most disturbed him, but he only was able to voice the fifth! What he fully **meant**, he couldn't articulate! This sudden insight saved me and the situation. I used my verbal deflectors: "I can see you're upset, and I would be, too, but I am here now, so let's be sure the house is secure, let me take a specific report of the missing items, and let me get the detectives working ASAP!" He, the victim, calmed down and later even apologized for his opening barrage of accusations. The call went smoothly after this.

I learned then, from this experience, an important principle: when people are upset, *"Words fly out, meanings follow behind."* As a Verbal Judo supervisor, you must educate your troops that when they encounter people under stress, which is most of the time, the words they (and You) initially hear are **not** what should be reacted to. Instead, effective officers will deflect such verbal attacks, and focus their response on the more accurate **meanings** behind the words. Officers or employees will have a far greater chance of bringing peace out of disorder if they learn and utilize this communication skill, and part of your job as a leader and supervisor is to teach this skill to your people.

It's important for you, the VJ supervisor, to use this principle yourself in your interactions with your troops and your superiors. An employee who confronts you, grumbling about the department or a certain policy, is actually telling you he needs some help in relating to the demands of his or her job. Do not focus on his negative words but rather on what these words can tell you about his needs. Rare is the person who can express what he truly means particularly if he or she is upset or rattled. Rather than react to the words, help your subordinate reveal to you the real need behind his words.

How? Use the most powerful tactic we know of, **Paraphrase**. Although I have talked about this in Chapter Ten of my book, *Verbal Judo: The Gentle Art of Persuasion* (Harper Collins, 1992), it is worth going over here because it is critically important for you as a supervisor and maturing leader. Paraphrase is the unique tactic of putting another's perceived **meaning** into your **words** and feeding it back to him to clarify what he is trying to tell you. Paraphrase is not repetition-you do not simply repeat what you heard-but it is a necessary redundancy that combines his **meaning**, as you define it, couched in your **words**, and then carefully fed back for affirmation or clarification. Do not use his words exactly for they may be emotionally "charged" and imprecise. Your words should be calmer and more rational-a paraphrase of what you believe you have heard in terms of **meaning**. Often when another hears his implied meaning coming back in a calmer manner and tone, he will immediately modify his original statement as he can now hear how perhaps badly he came off the first time around.

There are two "tricks" to effective paraphrase that you must be aware of and employ properly.

*One*, whenever you are paraphrasing, **be disinterested**! That is, deliver what you think he means as fairly and as impartially as possible, even if you feel his position is off-key or out of line. Any hint of judgment in your paraphrase will destroy the process and end in an antagonistic relationship.

**Two**, always use the **"Sword of Interruption"** to break in and take control of the encounter. When people are angry and upset, the quicker you can take positive control, the greater your chances of bringing reason and good sense to the encounter.

The moment you think you understand what the other means, break in with something like, "Whoa, let me see if I understand what you just said. Okay, you feel X because of Y? Would this be accurate?" This sentence literally closes people down, because you are now talking about their perceptions and feelings and giving every appearance of working with instead of against them, and you therefore begin to gain control over the encounter. It is the only way to interrupt someone and not generate resistance!

Be sure to use the correct **formula** for paraphrase. When you respond, put his **feelings first**, and his **reason or reasons** second, as in "Ok, so you feel X because of Y? Correct?"

The subject can then respond in several ways.

1. He can modify the feeling, but agree with the reason;
2. He can agree with the feeling but modify the reason; or
3. He can modify both.

Whatever the case, you have bought time for him to calm down a bit, as he listens to your feedback, and you now give him the opportunity to re-express his ideas in less emotionally charged language.

Consider this example. A subordinate confronts you in your office with these words:

*Let me tell you something! Everyone in this organization is trying to undermine my work here. Every time I turn around, someone is throwing another stumbling block in my way. This place is screwed!*

What is his **meaning**? Is "everyone" really doing this? Is it "every time"? Try a paraphrase. "Okay. Let me see if I have this right. You are feeling frustrated, even angry, because you believe people are purposely trying to undermine your work here? Am I understanding you correctly?"

The chances are the subordinate will modify his next statement to something like,

*No, I don't mean everyone, and I don't know if they are doing it on purpose, but I do know I feel frustrated by having people constantly question my work.*

Notice how much less "charged" his statement is, and how much more reasonable it now is. Another paraphrase will probably get you even closer to the truth. Perhaps someone, Mr. X, actually failed to work with the subordinate in a manner that helped him be successful, and now you have something you can suggest to help resolve the employee's frustration and move him in a more positive direction.

Notice that when the subordinate responded to your paraphrase, he admitted he was frustrated, but modified his reasons, which gave you some sense of what was really bothering

him. Had you not used paraphrase you might have been tempted
to react "naturally" and say something like,

> *You've got a bad attitude, you know that! People aren't out
> to get you! You are just paranoid. Shape it up! Don't whine
> to me!*

Such words would only heighten the problem. Be tactful, use
paraphrase to discover the meaning lying behind the angry words
so you can become who you have to be to help your employee
resolve his problem.

Try these two examples on your own.

> *The top-brass wants us to take all this training where new
> ideas are laid out, but when we try to use them and it
> doesn't go exactly right, we get no support up above.*

You feel _____ because _____,
True?

> *Most of these damn research and stat jobs take more time
> and effort than they are worth. I spend days working on
> these and no one pays any attention to them anyway. It's
> crap!*

You feel _____ because _____.
True?

As a leader and supervisor, the sooner you can tune into what
someone **means** rather than the **words** he is expressing, the
sooner you can be of real help in resolving conflict and getting
your people to work in greater harmony.

### 2. TWO PEOPLE = SIX IDENTITIES

Here is another surprising truth. When two people talk to one
another, there are at least six different identities striving for
dominance. There is **The Real Self**, of course, who you are given
your years and your total experience. This Self lies at our center
and is often hard to know. It is who we are, our values, the
totality of our experiences, our upbringing and acculturation. This

is the Self that psychologists try to reach and probe when we go for counseling. We tend to be aware of this Self only partly, and at times, and we often cover it over with protective devices to keep it safe from outside scrutiny. We know that at any time someone can say or do something that will "hit home" and make us flare up as we react to this often buried Self. Obviously, the more you know about your "real self" the better you can control such flare-ups. Again, this points out the necessity of knowing your weaknesses and controlling them by defining them as we mentioned earlier.

Next, we have the **Self as Seen by the Self**, our concept of ourselves as we would like to see ourselves. We constantly shape and reshape this concept as our world changes around us and as our sense of who we are changes with our promotions and our experiences. It is good to shape a confident self-image and project this outwardly as we interact with our colleagues. Indeed, we should not strive to see ourselves as elite, for example, to put others down rather than raise them up. How we interact with our people and what we do to them has a huge influence on how they see themselves. We should always strive to raise others' expectations of themselves, the real secret of motivation!

Despite whatever our inner misgivings and fears, we strive to put on a face to meet the faces we meet. We want others to see this face and to respond to it as we see it. When they do, we feel accepted and good. When they do not, we have a problem, and this leads us to our third self, the **Self as Seen by Others**.

How others see us is the crucial Self for acceptance and success. We know from experience, that whenever there is a conflict between how we see ourselves and how we are seen, **how we are seen dominates!**

How dangerous is this conflict? Very! Think how many people you know who believe they are coming across to others as X when in fact people see them as Y! Some people have no idea how they are truly seen by others, and they continue on, interacting with others, and failing at every turn. We at the Verbal Judo Institute have encountered many supervisors who believe they are seen as respected men of vision and talent when in fact they are universally hated and despised! I, personally, often have wondered how this is possible. Do they not awake in the middle of the night and know they are hated? How can they not know how people truly see and feel about them?

Ego has much to do with it. Some supervisors are so distant from their peers and colleagues, so filled with their own importance and position, they are truly blind to the perceptions of others. Some even claim they do not care what others think. Surely working under such an illusion must be a terrible daily experience, as only a certified sociopath or narcissist truly doesn't care about what others think of him or her.

Those of us who are in touch with our Selves in a manner that is reality-based and not ego-centered, know that if we are not seen as we desire we should be, we are motivated to change the errant perceptions of others quickly for our benefit and the benefit of those we are in contact with. If our troops, for example, think we are unfair and biased, we are, and that is how they will respond to us until we successfully unravel the mistaken perception and replace it with one that is accurate and reality-based. The VJ communications expert will readjust his or her employees' or subordinates' thinking (and therefore behavior) by changing or readjusting the way we act in their presence.

Remember the chameleon. Become who you must be to handle the people you supervise. If we do not, we are doomed to be labeled based on errant perceptions.

### 3.  93% OF OUR EFFECTIVENESS LIES IN DELIVERY!

How many times have you heard "it's not what you say, it's how you say it that counts"? We know from research that our mode of **delivery** is approximately 93% of our effectiveness. **Content**, or the message we are actually sending, accounts for approximately 7 to 10% of our effectiveness, if we are accurate in our communication language. Those of us who feel we are most always right and most always know what we are saying is true, will find this fact a bit surprising. To be sure, if we are dealing with facts only, being right can be proved. But in the Art of Persuasion, or in matters that can be debated, content is not necessarily powerful. You must be right, yes, but unless you can convey your message effectively being right might as well be wrong.

We know that **Voice** is 33-40% of our effectiveness. **Voice** is our "verbal personality," our Self heard by others, our tape recorded voice. It is not how we hear ourselves, but how we are heard by others that has a dramatic impact.

The most potentially damaging quality of voice is our TONE. **Tone** may be better defined as our **perceived attitude**, and that is most accurately defined as the words people hear **at the end of our spoken sentence**. Tone is the most deadly word in the English language! Tone has caused more anger, misunderstanding, and conflict than any word known to man. Given our sentences, people will add to what they hear as implied by Tone at the end of what is said. You say with biting sarcasm to an employee, "Didn't you get it the first time?" What the employee hears is "idiot" at the end of your sentence. Tone gives our inner feelings away every time. We know that whenever role and voice conflict, voice will dominate. Regard role as the "what" of your sentence or the action. Content is worth only 7-10%. Voice is 33-40% of your overall impact, and hence, if your tone is negative, your impact will be negative, regardless of your intentions.

The secret of success, therefore, is to **harmonize Voice and Role!** If someone asks you to "play the role" of guidance counselor, for example, your voice must match the role. You must sound as if you are giving counsel, not criticizing or judging. We play many roles everyday, and we should always make our Voice match the selected Role. I have heard many supervisors say things like, "Hey, I helped him and he took it the wrong way. What can I do?" First, you can recognize that you are the problem! If he took it the wrong way, you most likely delivered the message poorly. Second, you should have seen, at the time of delivery, you were not coming across as you may have intended. Watching the face of the person across from you can allow for swift changes in tone and words so misunderstandings can be avoided.

As a supervisor, you need not only to heed this advice, but also to pass it along to your employees who so very often do the right thing but too often say what they don't mean using abrupt, insensitive language. Think of all the complaints that come across your desk. My own research shows that 90% of the complaints that come into a police department, for example, are tonally related! "The officer was rude; the officer was condescending; the officer didn't care; the officer treated us like we were second-rate citizens." Rarely do police officers draw complaints solely on what they **did**; it's almost always on **how they sounded when they did it**. An officer or employee that allows his personal feelings to be heard in his dialogue via Tone will always get the short end of the stick. Thompson's Law, **make the voice adapt to the role!**

Fit the voice to the role, be the verbal chameleon by "chameleoning up" to the situation. If you don't, the tone of your voice will betray you.

I backed an officer up one night on a multiple traffic accident. The woman who caused the accident was written a ticket, advised regarding insurance procedures, and let go. The next day she filed a complaint with the Chief, alleging that the officer had called her "an idiot!" The Chief called me in and asked me about her allegation. I said, truthfully, that the officer had said no such thing. But I do know the officer thought she was stupid and he let her know this through his tone of voice when he addressed her. This example shows so clearly how powerful tone can be. The woman truly believed the officer used those offensive words, and probably believes it to this day. Nothing makes enemies quicker than loose lips that allow inner feelings to come through in the tone of the officer. School your employees and subordinates to harmonize their Voices and Tones with the Roles they are asked to play, or which they elect to play. The voice is your tool of success if used correctly. Chameleon up!

Other elements of voice are Pace, Pitch, and Modulation.

**Pace** refers to the speed of the voice-slow to fast.

**Pitch** relates to high or low, loud or soft. Both of these are extremely important as they relate to effective communication. Leaders and supervisors need to learn to listen to voice changes. If an employee's voice begins to speed up, he is becoming excited, perhaps ready to explode into action. If the voice noticeably begins to slow down, the employee may be coming to a decision, perhaps to strike or to flee or simply to comply. Similarly, changes in a voice's Pitch can signal internal changes that a leader needs to pay attention to.

**Modulation** is extremely important, for it is the rhythm and inflection of your sentence. In English, much meaning is conveyed by inflection. Consider the example, "I never said he stole the money." If you stress the "I" it means, you didn't say it but someone else did! If you stress the word "said," it means you are implying he may have. To emphasize the word "he" suggests someone else most certainly did steal the money, and if you emphasize the last word, "money," it suggests he stole something else all together! Much of our real, inner feelings are revealed by how we modulate a sentence, and we can lose a lot of credibility and good will if we are careless in how we say things.

Even more important than controlling one's voice properly is the ability to control one's **Body Language**, or other non-verbals. We know that just as Role and Voice must harmonize, so must **Voice** and **Other Non-Verbals**, or **ONVs**, are approximately 50-60% of our total impact on others! You can make your voice sound pleasant, for example, when you do not particularly like someone, but your non-verbals will give your real feelings away. Whenever people see a contradiction between your voice and your ONVs, they believe the ONVs, and so do you! Some people pick up on ONV's quicker than others. My wife is a good example; she is very quick to see a roll of the eye that belies what I might be saying. A teacher once rolled her eyes at a question my wife asked about our son in class, and my wife immediately reacted to that and told her, "Don't you roll your eyes at me...." What the teacher had been saying was appropriate (content), and her voice was neutral to pleasant, but her eyes gave her away, and she got righteously slammed! No matter what the teacher said from then on, my wife left the session believing the teacher really didn't want to hear our views. **ONVs** are more than **content** and **voice** put together. They are subtle and not-so-subtle responses and reactions people simply pick up in an instant! Chameleon up!

Too often, we do not know how we alert people non-verbally! I was in Oregon several years ago now training the Oregon State Police. As I drove along the road going to a class in the eastern part of the state I noticed an OSP officer had pulled over a semi truck. I stopped off to one side and decided to watch the contact. I had my video camera with me, so I videoed the scene as it went down. The trooper got out of his car and literally swaggered up the road to the truck cab. He was a short, muscular officer, who rolled from side to side as he approached the driver. I am sure the driver saw what I would have seen approaching in his mirrors— trouble en route! You could tell from the walk!

Four days later I had that officer in class. I showed the video without any warning, and the officer did NOT recognize himself! When I told him he was the trooper in the film clip he said, "Can't be! I don't walk like that!" Funny. Funny also that the trooper was one of their best! He had a superb arrest record and was highly thought of, yet he got complaints and never understood why. When he watched the tape, over and over, he saw what others saw. The tape made it clear. Just his walk made people bristle! He just didn't know it. It was just his manner of walking. He had to change, he had to chameleon up, and he did, and I later heard the complaints stopped.

Because of your position of assigned power over others, you as a supervisor must be very careful about the messages you send non-verbally. The upshot of this communication section is a dreadful truth: 93% of your effectiveness lies in your delivery style! You must make your **body language** harmonize with your **role** and **voice**, and only when all three are in harmony can you have successful communication. For police, ONV's are closer to 60% because of the uniform and the gun. Delivery Style, 33% minimum for VOICE and 60% plus for ONV, add up to 93%. In some cases, ONV's can account for 100% if they are negative enough.

One example of such an ONV is the supervisor who during a conversation with a subordinate flicks his or her eyes up at the clock. This is a technique taught by some courses to draw attention to time available to the supervisor...the message really sent is "I have no more time for either you or this. Move on!" The subordinate involved will most likely shut down any further meaningful dialogue and depart feeling as if he doesn't matter, and his issue or problem is unimportant. The result of this ONV is often fewer and fewer visits with the supervisor, and an ever-narrowing communications pipeline.

And this is when the real problems begin.

The importance of being flexible in your delivery style cannot be overstated. If supervisors want to be effective with their people they must learn to regard delivery style as a crucial tactical skill. It is not something many think about as they start their careers, but as you can now see, it is the defining skill of success with people. Take pride in your ability to "chameleon up," verbally and non-verbally, because it is the only way to be successful and to get people to do what you want them to do. If you care about your ideas, your positions, your points, you will care enough to **"dress"** them appropriately so others can accept them. You will see how important this is when we discuss the different Personality Styles people naturally have and you see how each style must be ad-dressed differently given the differing ways each Style processes information.

So there you have it, the three Street Truths of communication, each significantly important to your success with people as a leader and supervisor. Be smarter, and hence more tactical, by knowing and obeying the truth that people never say precisely what they mean. Learn to encourage people to clarify their real meanings (feelings and concerns) before you respond. Know, too, that how you are seen (Self as Seen by Others) will affect your entire career, continuously. Be alert to the feedback you get and be flexible enough to modify and "chameleon up" as necessary and appropriate. And, finally, never forget that no matter how right you may be in your thoughts and ideas, how you deliver them will make all the difference. Don't let yourself be trapped by ego or rigidity. If your ideas are good, respect them enough to give them the appropriate dress and delivery style. Be aware of your own ONVs as well as those of your subordinates and employees. Detecting and interpreting them correctly is the trademark of the communication professional.

## CHAPTER FIVE

# THE "HOOK DOWN" THEORY OF VERBAL JUDO SUPERVISION

---

Too many supervisors have lost touch with their people on the street, if they were in touch with them to begin with. Were I to define the greatest voiced concern heard over the past twenty years of teaching Verbal Judo, it is that officers and employees believe their higher echelon people are out of touch with the real job of street work! Too many administrators and supervisors pursue a course of professional distancing. They convince themselves they are now "organizational-motivated." They intentionally forget what it's like to work the streets or on the shop floors. They will, if pushed, state they don't care about these things because they see their jobs as being "above all that." The swiftest response is "I don't have time for EVERYTHING, you know!" Right or wrong, police officers at the street level believe their managements to be out of touch and in fact employees and subordinates across our land likewise feel the same way. Today there exists a very real, very destructive "Us" versus "Them" culture in the American workplace. Administrators blame employees and their unions and associations; employees blame their management teams; unions and associations blame both sides of the coin; city and county councils blame factors "out of our control." The list of fault finding goes on and on.

When we discuss this in VJ supervisory classes, we often hear, "Look, I spent ten years on the streets, I know what's it's like. As a supervisor I have another kind of work now. Paperwork is crucial to our success!" When we hear this excuse for flying a desk, we know there is a degree of truth to the statement, but ten years on the streets, ten years ago, means very little to those working on the frontlines here and now. The rush for many to get "off the streets" and into administration is killing both private and public sector workplaces. Unless very carefully modeled and managed by the senior leadership of a business or agency, the result is supervisors with very little positive, productive work experience being promoted into positions of authority where their lack of credibility is so great to begin with, they cannot hope to function effectively, much less be successful. Police officers, for example, are taught early on that there is no real career progression in law enforcement if one stays too long on the streets. Longevity as a street cop will only hurt your career advancement, they are told. The result of this *lie* results in street officers chaffing at their supervisors' bits until they become a supervisor themselves. Once in the position of authority to change the negative culture they were raised in, they conveniently forget where they came from and move blindly ahead, doing exactly the kind of things they once complained their supervisors did.

For example, in one organization we are aware of a well-trained and experienced street officer with several years of detective experience, was successfully promoted to the rank of sergeant. When he began his new career as a supervisor he met with his team of officers and shared with them his vision for how much better their professional lives were going to be now that he was in a position to make a difference. In short order, however, the new sergeant began behaving like those other sergeants in his department. He began finding fault with one officer, then another. He began turning minor deficiencies into major events. He began backing the administration and his fellow sergeants over his team. Soon his officers realized he'd abandoned them despite putting his best foot forward upon promotion. They began fighting back through their union and personal legal repre-sentation. They began fighting back on the job, doing only "what was required." This frightened the new sergeant. The uprising on his team drew attention to his performance from both the mid- and upper-management groups in the department. "Can't you control your shift?" he was asked by his patrol captain and fellow sergeants. His chief, likewise, counseled him as to how he might better prove he was worthy of his new stripes. Over the coming months the new sergeant tried to please his peers and bosses by singling out individual officers and taking them to task. Each time his efforts were stonewalled or turned around on him by an officer body well versed in protecting its members from just such prosecutorial supervision. In the bigger picture his team's efforts on the street dropped significantly. The officers were too busy protecting themselves to spend quality time protecting the Public.

After less than two years as a sergeant a need for the city to lay off one of its police supervisors resulted in the newest ser-geant getting the axe. He discovered the overall officer body in the department felt little or no sympathy for his situation. He'd betrayed their trust and sought to destroy at least two careers in his misguided effort to integrate himself with what he believed was his new peer group (the other sergeants). He thought his job as a supervisor was to curry favor, to save his own career. The final result was the departure of the sergeant from not only his department but from the area where he'd lived and raised his family for over a decade. He found work elsewhere but the cost he paid was a high one for everyone involved.

How could he have saved his professional integrity with his officers and still become an effective supervisor within his department and community? First, he needed to return to the primitive but true premise that supervisors must be out with their people. They must lead from the front—always—and they must work with, and not simply oversee, their people. Over the years I have developed and taught a theory I call the **"Hook Down"** theory of supervision. Simply stated, it says this: **the higher you go up the ranks, the deeper you must hook down to the street level, proportionately!** An officer spends 100% of his or her time working the streets. The moment that officer is promoted to Sergeant, it becomes an 80%-20% job, if done correctly. That means, eighty percent of the new supervisor's time should be spent on the streets, backing his people, evaluating his people, teaching his people, and overseeing their operations. Twenty percent will be office time and paperwork. Indeed, the Sergeant level is, by definition, a first-line supervisory job. Ideally, his patrol car **is** his office! In far too many departments, offices, businesses, and corporations the reverse of this formula is the rule upon promotion.

Our own experience has shown us that indeed many sergeants and first line supervisors / managers understand they must stay connected with their workforce. They see their closeness with their subordinates as the reason they see continued success on the streets. Still, unless upper management is healthy in its outlook this form of positive, productive supervision cannot exist for any length of time. The military and police sergeant is truly the operations leader of his unit or shift, and hence cannot be off the streets for any appreciable time. Whenever we hear complaints from a frontline work group about sergeants, they almost always hinge on the sergeant not being on the streets, not being with his troops. The only exception to this principle might be the purely "administrative" sergeant. Bear in mind, far too many chiefs and corporate leaders *insist* their new supervisors get off the streets or off the assembly lines and into offices. Their reasons are misguided and self-serving. They find power in dividing and conquering their subordinates and they maintain power by creating diversion within their organizations.

Make a note! An overwhelming number of police chiefs, sheriffs, office managers, and corporate CEOs have forsaken the sacred trust placed in them and pursue strictly their own agendas and careers. They prey upon the weaknesses of the system and upon the frailties of their organization. Pitting supervisors against those supervised is an age-old means of internal warfare that ultimately destroys careers, lives, and organizations. This trend is rooted in an "It's all about me" belief system of leadership and supervision that is and remains dysfunctional to the extreme.

When you reach the level of Lieutenant in a law enforcement scenario the percentage of street to office time changes, for indeed this level is heavy with paperwork and planning concerns. Even so the Lieutenant cannot afford to be distant, or to distance himself from his troops. Depending on the size of the department, the percentages may vary, but whatever the case, they should be as close to 30%-70% as possible. A Lieutenant should be on the streets, in uniform, thirty percent of the time, monitoring his Sergeants and answering some basic calls to relieve the strain on the patrol officers and to keep his skills fresh. When I mention such figures in classes, I usually get laughter and guffaws from the troops who quickly inform me, "That will never happen in my department!"

We ask, "But shouldn't it?" What a difference such a proactive presence would make! But how can we get chiefs and sheriffs and private sector upper management to institute and mature such an idea? It cannot be mandated, as forced leadership is no leadership at all. The senior-most leader of any department, organization, or business must first model this management theme and then teach it from *the top down*. It must be taught, reinforced, encouraged, monitored, critiqued, and then promoted daily as how the organization is to be run *from the top down*. Those who can't or don't get it should be moved out or back into the ranks. Attainable and trainable goals are set for performance and achievement by all levels of leadership, management, and supervision. The workforce is engaged by the frontline supervisory body with this dynamic method of mentoring and maturing the average employee and subordinate. It is the frontline supervisor who then models, teaches, trains and encourages his or her subordinates to be "hooked up"; brought up to the level of daily and long-term performance identified by the senior-most management team as the criteria for success in terms of the organization's set goals.

Just think how different the new sergeant's professional life might have been if his peers and senior supervisor/chief would have developed their organization to reflect the above approach to supervision as opposed to the self-serving, petty boot-licking he determined as being his only way of fitting in and succeeding!

Without exception, every police lieutenant has been praised for **being** out with his troops, on the street. Troops, cops, and employees love such leadership, and they thirst for more! If a department or organization believes in Community Policing, as many do, what better way to advance such policing than to have the higher ranks answering calls for service? Admittedly, we do not want our older supervisors handling the hot calls on a primary level. That is what the young "dawgs" are for—quick, rapid, and youthful response! But quality supervisors regardless of their jobs or profession must be encouraged *from the top down* to monitor from the immediate background. This so they will be capable of appraising their peoples' performance and do so fairly and effectively, invoking respect from those whose actions they are charged with responsibility for.

We have seen too many instances of a "boss" interfering needlessly in a police call or employee project just because he can while at the same time being absent from the physical perspective. This does nothing but anger employees and subordinates and anger erodes morale not to mention continued reliable work products!

Indeed, here is a principle that we recommend all supervisors follow:

> **The more mundane a task a supervisor performs for his troops, the greater his credibility in the eyes of his troops!**

A cold burglary report, a cat in a tree, checking out an abandoned vehicle, sweeping the shop floor, cleaning the communal bathroom, buying lunch and bringing it in for those working through their lunch: all such symbolic and heartfelt actions and others like them provide ample opportunities for the leader, the manager, the supervisor to take some pressure off his troops and to demonstrate he or she is a part of the real team effort at hand.

I'll never forget the lieutenant that came by during one of my DUI stops one day. As I was wrapping up the stop and subsequent arrest he told me, "Go with your prisoner, I'll do the car inventory report and get it to you at the department." I was both relieved to get underway and appreciative that he, at his rank, would so casually offer to help me out. My respect for him and the effort I put into the rest of the case went sky-high, which I believe he knew would be the effect of his action.

Then there was the captain who came by one night when I had a suspect in custody for an alleged shooting. He said, "Take the prisoner in, I'll stand by his vehicle until the detectives get here." It was pouring rain, and yet here he was, putting on a raincoat, and standing by the car so I could get to the station and complete the processing of the suspect! Such actions are memorable to any of us who have worked the street. We would walk through Hell itself to work for such people. I knew these two supervisors and leaders cared what I did out there. That translated into respect for the department's senior-most leadership, and for myself and how I went about doing my job each day. Leaders lead by their example and new leaders are created by the examples they are given when they are in the ranks, at whatever job they have.

This philosophy truly seems difficult for some people to grasp. I once taught a supervisory class in which a captain, after hearing my Hook Down Theory, returned to class the next day to relate to me how he had followed my advice. It seems he had been driving home from the class and as he crossed a bridge over a creek he saw a man standing on the railing, apparently preparing to jump into the swift waters below. The captain told me he immediately radioed for a patrol unit to check the bridge area for the man. He then proceeded home. He thought he had done what I suggested the day before! Imagine! Going home rather than stopping and handling the call himself! His perception of participating, of leading, of perhaps saving a life, was to personally use a radio to call a subordinate to the scene and then to go right home! How he was viewed, after the officer arrived to look for the would-be jumper, is perhaps predictable.

Other supervisors have told me that though they agree the Hook Down Theory has merit, and indeed they would like to spend some more time with their troops on the streets, their chiefs and sheriffs won't allow it. "That's not your job," they are told, and they fear reprisals if they were to join their troops on patrol. Some are further warned, "It's not your job to be close to the troops!" This view comes from the philosophy that if you are close to your troops you cannot effectively supervise and discipline them. Unspoken is the view that once becoming a supervisor or manager, one becomes somehow "elite," or better than what they were before as an employee or frontline subordinate. This view is wrong and serves only the Ego and not the organization. In larger departments, the air can be quite rarified on the higher levels. Many supervisors, as they struggle for oxygen at the higher altitudes, readily admit their happiest times were when they were on patrol. Right thinking and right actions come from *the top down*, not from the bottom up. Excuses are like anal openings...everyone has one. Leaders don't make excuses for their inability to lead...they "cowboy up" and lead!

Far too many supervisors have a twisted idea of what the job entails and perhaps you've experienced this kind of management style. Consider the following from a highway patrol officer, one well regarded, with many honors and awards.

> *I am confident I am not what you would call a "problem officer." On the contrary, I do a good professional job and I have a number of commendations in my personnel file to show for it. However, years of disrespectful and condescending treatment by supervisors can insidiously wear a man down. I have seen this gradual de-motivation process infect other officers as well as myself at the hands of supervisors who have no idea how to lead, but they think they know how to manage. The finest supervisors I have worked with lead their men into battle by example whereas the "wimp" supervisors attempt to manage, primarily by way of criticism of their men, from behind the security of a desk. They are always there to point out what is wrong in painful detail, but rarely take equal notice of a difficult job well done. The wimps risk nothing whereas the respected leaders do not ask their troops to do anything they would not readily do themselves.*

He goes further:

*I recently investigated an injury accident involving an overturned tractor-trailer that required blocking the entire highway to clear. It was pouring rain and I was the only local patrol out. I had a real mess on my hands, and yet only a few miles away, a sergeant and lieutenant sat on their butts in the patrol office and would not respond to help me despite my calls for assistance. Fortunately a local deputy responded. When I returned to the office after the accident was cleared, I asked why neither the sergeant nor the lieutenant came to the scene. I was told that they felt I could handle it myself and that their jobs were to supervise, not to direct traffic at accidents.*

This officer said his entire career was filled with stories like this one, and over the years we have heard other officers relate all too similar examples of supervisors not being there for them when needed. To distance yourself from your employees and subordinates is to lose credibility and knowledge, so why do so many behave this way? Old beliefs and *mis*management styles die hard, and one of the most dangerous old beliefs and styles is the one where you as a supervisor and leader hide yourself away with a sharp pencil and sharp tongue, at the expense of your charges' respect and belief that you are fit to direct their actions and careers.

How many captains, majors, and assistant chiefs do we see on the streets? How many mid-level supervisors work the floors now and then? Few. A police captain, for example, should "hook down" to the streets around 20%, and the higher ups at least 10%. A captain could profitably spend eight to ten hours a week out with his troops, if only riding with one or another to learn how his or her men and women are feeling about the job. As the captain develops trust—he's not in the field to spy but to help and debrief—he will develop a much better sense of the needs of the department and actually see how the policies and procedures he helped develop are working, in reality, on the streets. This translates into first-hand knowledge and avoids the pitfalls of hearsay and distortion from other middle management people, many of who tell their superiors what they think they want to hear rather than the truth!

To witness an assistant chief or chief actually on the streets is an uplifting sight rarely seen, much less experienced. Say what you want about Chief Daryl Gates of the LAPD, his men and women loved him precisely because he was out there, on the streets, with his troops. I once saw him arrive at a scene around 4 a.m. to help his officers on a block where a gang shooting had taken place. He helped keep spectators away while his officers set up the crime scene. When he was asked why he was there, he said he heard the call on the scanner, couldn't sleep, so he thought he would come to the scene to see if he could be of some assistance! On the day he retired, under pressure, I saw tears in the eyes of his officers. When I asked several how they felt about him, they said, "He was one of us." No greater compliment could an officer give a Chief or any supervisor!

Contrast this fine example with one my co-author once witnessed. A well-known vagrant had perched himself comfortably in an area where he could overlook the river and visit with his friends. The chief of police elected to respond to the call knowing the area was off-limits due to the city's storage of some valuable equipment in the building the vagrant had chosen to occupy. My co-author likewise responded to back the chief up, knowing in part the department's senior administrator rarely handled calls. "When I arrived I settled back and watched as both men began to argue about why the violator needed to leave the premises," recounts my co-author. "Soon the chief began taking a hard line, threatening this and that with no good effect. The vagrant easily held his own, challenging the chief's position and directives and arguments like a well-seasoned boxer does an unsure opponent.

"It finally got to the point where I gently interjected myself and encouraged the chief to clear the area. I offered to take over. He did so but reluctantly. When he left I spent some time just listening to what the vagrant had to say. When the right moment offered itself I was able to quietly motivate the vagrant to move on, and in a manner that left him with his dignity."

What if, for some reason, a supervisor is not able to get out on the streets, either because of health reasons or pressure from above? Is it still possible to stay in close contact with the troops or employees? Yes, by modifying the Hook Down Principle. If, for example, you are a senior supervisor or manager you can read some of the reports filed by your officers and then, over the next day or two, get out of your office and search out the officers so you can comment positively on their street performance. Think of the morale booster it would be if an officer suddenly found himself face to face with a captain who said, "Hey, John, I really appreciate the way you handled that call the other night at the Four Seasons Tavern! Made some good arrests and managed to avoid stirring people up any more than you had to. Good work!" Not only does the officer go away feeling good but he also learns his often unseen superior is aware of his work and overseeing his performance. That not only encourages a subordinate but also serves to keep him or her on the straight and narrow!

True leadership power is **contact power**, and it is in the supervisor's best interest to stay in close contact with his people in a proactive and positive manner to develop this kind of earned authority. Without it you become as my co-author's chief did that afternoon: out of balance, out of touch, out of focus, and asked to leave so the real cops can get the job done before you screw up their day.

If you are reading this and are a seasoned supervisor but sense you have lost some credibility with your troops or subordinates, the best way back is to follow the Hook Down Theory. **Reintegrate** yourself with your people by **reconnecting** yourself to the job that your people do. Be positive, do the little things, ask to help if you can and do whatever is asked of you to the best of your ability. Let your people know you care, you are there for, and with, them, and you can be trusted. If you are a new supervisor, follow our theory each and every day. Doing so will create a leadership "glove" for you that will carry you and your career through the best and worst times. A good department is a team, and a team works together on all levels. **Distance and separation** are the evil twins of garbage leadership and ineffective management. Avoid them at all costs!

## CHAPTER SIX

# THE FOUR LEVELS OF EXPERTISE

O ne of the reasons the **Hook Down Principle** is so necessary for your success as a supervisor is, it helps ensure that you keep your fingers on the pulse of your organization. In any organization, people tend to fall into one or more of the four levels of expertise we in Verbal Judo consider as organizational norm:

Unconscious Incompetence
Conscious Incompetence
Unconscious Competence
Conscious Competence

The **Conscious Competent** is the highest-level performer, but this is a very difficult level to achieve, and impossible without first-hand knowledge of operations in the field. It is important that you, the supervisor, know how these four levels apply to you, and just as important, that you use them to analyze the men and women under your command and then use this analysis to better your organization as a whole.

The **Unconscious Incompetent** is the most dangerous level in any organization, for this person is wholly incompetent in his or her daily work and worse, is wholly unaware of it! This is the employee who, when you reprimand him for some mistake, is always surprised, even angry, that you even brought their lack of performance up! The typical Unconscious Incompetent's response is, *"I've always done it this way,"* and this in itself marks their lack of awareness. In management this is the supervisor who, when reading this book for example, fails to recognize himself in those areas he or she is incompetent or severely lacking. This is the supervisor who is universally hated by his troops and is totally, almost blissfully unaware of it! He believes his performance as a supervisor and leader is superb! Make a note. Minimal expertise, combined with inaccurate self-assessment, spells disaster! This level of employee and/or supervisor is most often impossible to cure and you do all involved a favor by carefully and properly educating such a person as to why they are encouraged to find work elsewhere before they are terminated for cause.

An example of Unconscious Incompetent was found in one department where a officer found himself promoted to a newly created administrative captain's position. He would remain in this position until his retirement, doing little more than carrying out the edicts of his chief and overseeing the patrol sergeants and officers below him. Never a rising star in the department as a patrol officer, the captain was even less impressive as an administrator. He became known for his personal bias toward some officers and sergeants, while at the same time overlooking the errors and misbehavior of those he felt comfortable with. His conduct of internal investigations most always led to union challenges, and most of these challenges led to victories for the officers involved and a black eye for the department. The captain, if you asked him, sincerely believed he was a model police administrator. Everything that went wrong during his watch was always someone else's fault! He never "got it" and no one ever felt it important enough to honestly inform him that he was, essentially, an Unconscious Incompetent.

The **Conscious Incompetent** is the next level of employee or supervisor. Indeed, all of us find ourselves in this category at times. Most of us realize we have weaknesses in dealing with people or in handling one or more aspects of a job, so we are aware of our failings and most often seek to address these in a positive, constructive manner. The most natural thing to do as a Conscious Incompetent is to mask our incompetence or avoid doing those tasks that reveal our incompetence to others. It is natural for human beings to want to hide their weaknesses from themselves and others. Seven out of ten people tend to handle their professional shortcomings this way. We know the path to failure is built on covered-over weaknesses! The ancient Samurai warriors teach otherwise. These ancient warriors taught that Strength is built on recognized weaknesses! To admit a weakness is a strength because now, having defined it, one can set about correcting it!

The Peter Principle illustrates precisely this natural tendency to cover and avoid shortcomings as one climbs the ladder of promotion. As the employee is promoted and more demands and responsibilities are assigned, he or she eventually reaches the point where any successfully hidden weaknesses suddenly erupt into view with failure an oncoming event. If one continuously makes weak areas stronger, there is no reason for the Peter Principle to become a factor in one's career. One reaches his or her level of incompetence if one allows, or is **conscious**, such areas of incompetence exist and does **nothing** about it!

One trait of the Conscious Incompetent is to blame others for continual failure. The Conscious Incompetent **knows** he or she is weak and actively seeks to create situations, find fall guys, and cultivate strong political ties with the higher-ups to deflect attention away from his shortcomings, errors, mistakes, poor performance, and outright bungles. The Conscious Incompetent often becomes a political animal; a cunning, backstabbing creature intent each day on keeping the charade alive that says, "I'm really quite good at what I do!" Conscious Incompetents must be swiftly identified and can be saved from themselves with proper supervision and careful nurturing by a senior supervisor or leader.

The Unconscious Competent is the next professional level and it is a very high level indeed! This is the worker who day in and day out does the job well, without giving it much conscious thought. He or she has "blood knowledge" of the job; it comes naturally and flows easily. Like muscle memory, the worker does quality work almost unconsciously. Whatever training the worker has taken, whatever the accomplishments of his or her success in the work environment, they all flow into one continuous and nearly flaw-free operation. It all looks easy; they just do it!

Many management experts regard this level as the highest of professional levels, but it is not. Though high in expertise, such persons are lacking in terms of realistic self-assessment and therein lies the crucial weakness of this level. Employers often do not know why what these employees do works so well for them. Such people, though high in skill, are ripe for the Peter Principle. Why? Because this level of employee lacks **the knowledge of how they do what they do best**. Therefore they cannot train and teach others how to emulate their performance and they will later bump into levels of incompetence without knowing why or how they got there.

Knowing how to do a job well is not the same as being able to teach another! To teach, one must be a **Conscious Competent,** one who not only can do the job well, but who **knows how he does what he does when he does what he does well!**

Without a doubt, the highest professional level is the **Conscious Competent,** or the employee and/or supervisor who possesses both a high level of expertise AND a high level of self-assessment! The great supervisor must be wiser than his people; he must not only be competent at what he or she does, but equally adept at teaching the crucial skills of job competence to the troops. People look to their supervisors to provide verifiable paths to success. If, therefore, you are successful in what you do, take stock of how you became successful. What steps did you take? What philosophy did you embrace? What advantages did you avail yourself of and what pitfalls did you learn to avoid? In short, what accounts for your success? Go so far as to list and define your own personal history.

For some of you, this will be a hard assignment because you are the **Unconscious Competent**. But you needn't stay in this category; you can go back through your history and reconstruct the steps that got you where you are and then move forward. Once you have some clear sense of how you did it, how you made it, you can help those below you find their way more quickly and efficiently. The knowledge you pass on to others becomes your legacy. Help your troops move to higher levels of competence, perhaps even surpassing your own level. Remember, the great Masters and Teachers had one goal: to get their students to go beyond them.

By carefully analyzing the four levels of employee and supervisor competence we can begin to re-create any organization we are members of. We know it is important to identify the Unconscious Incompetent and nicely but swiftly weed him out. We understand the Conscious Incompetent is afraid of his own professional shadow and with proper identification, a realistic assessment, quality re-training and consistent supervision he or she can evolve into a Conscious Competent in good standing. The Unconscious Competent is that steady workhorse who just gets it done day in and day out and we as leaders and supervisors love this guy! But if we understand him at all we know it is important for the organization as a whole to learn WHY he is so competent, and then reveal this mystery's solution to him as well as those around him for the benefit of all. The Unconscious Competent is the most swift to attain Conscious Competency if matured properly by his senior leadership. We need this person to become enlightened so the organization can grow stronger!

Finally, the **Conscious Competent** must be properly identified at whatever level we find him and then moved up through the ranks with careful, thoughtful grooming and preparation. He is the hope for the future and the example others in the organization must look to for inspiration and confidence. The Conscious Competent becomes a searcher for those other levels discussed, someone who becomes a teacher and then mentor. We must staff our most basic work teams with Conscious Competent leadership and supervision. And then work up the chain until its links from top to bottom reflect a dynamic and consistent competence of performance day in and day out.

We once heard a police chief bemoan his belief that "you can't fire someone for incompetence!" What hogwash. You can identify incompetence and then begin to either correct or eliminate it in your workforce. Incompetence leads to mistakes, and some of these mistakes will be made unknowingly (Unconscious Incompetent: "I didn't know!") or in full knowledge (Conscious Incompetent: "I hope I don't get caught!"). Harboring the incompetent in either category leads to all manner of disaster in an organization. You can terminate an employee or demote a supervisor for being incompetent at his job. You, as a Conscious Competent supervisor or leader, need only to be able to articulate and document WHY such disciplinary action MUST be taken for the good of the Order. To allow incompetence a berth in your organization is in itself a sign of incompetence at the highest level of responsibility. It is also the sign of a moral and ethical coward.

In every chapter of this book we seek to make you **Consciously Competent**. In the next chapter we will help you define your communication style so you will have the ability to flex that style effectively as you encounter people and their unique personality traits and behaviors. Once you become aware of how you actually process communication, you can more knowingly make decisions on how you want to deliver information to others, and as you will remember, delivery is 93% of your success as a supervisor and leader!

## CHAPTER SEVEN

# YOUR COMMUNICATION PROFILE

---

This will be an eye-opening chapter for you. If you believe in the "Hook Down Theory" of supervision we defined in Chapter Five, and if you want to be more consciously competent, as we discussed in Chapter Six, then this **Profile** will measurably help you relate more effectively to the different personalities of your troops and will equally aid you in knowing more about yourself and your strengths and weaknesses as a communicator. This Profile will tell you about yourself. How you process information, what you value when you listen and what you do not. Have you ever wondered why you find yourself frustrated when dealing with some troops and not others? Do you ever wonder why you are able to relate so smoothly to some, and yet bristle and chaff at others? This Profile of your style will help you understand why some people are easier for you to communicate with and others very difficult.

I first experienced this Profile in 1991 with Maxine Macintyre Hammond when she and I were teaching supervisors at L. A. County Sheriff's department. There are many instruments one could use to define one's communication style, but most are very complicated. You can literally take three to five day courses on this subject, and indeed, if you have the time, you should avail yourself of this opportunity. Companies such as Wilson Learning, based in Santa Fe, N.M., can provide such extensive training. But for a clean, clear, and precise definition of how you relate to others, this instrument is the best I know of; it is easy to take and easy to use with your own people.

As an instrument, the following questionnaire and scoring sheet will help you do a number of things better than you ever have before.

First, it will provide a very clear **definition** of who you are, both under normal conditions and under more stressful conditions. Earlier in the book we talked about the importance of knowing your weaknesses, and controlling them by defining, naming, and thus owning them. Here we go a bit farther, defining your strengths and predilections as a communicator. We each have a "style" of processing information, and the more we know about it the better we can manage it and flex it when we meet people of differing styles. Your Conscious Competent quotient will rise dramatically once you have this information.

Second, knowing the four basic styles and their characteristics will markedly improve your ability to **"read others"** with whom you interact. The ideal condition would be to give this Profile to your subordinates and then discuss the results with them, indicating the strengths of their style and the potential weaknesses of that style as they encounter others, including yourself, who may be different. But just knowing the styles and their defining characteristics will help you to understand your troops more readily and help you adjust your style accordingly.

Third, being aware of stylistic differences will enable you to be **more knowledgeable** about who to assign tasks and positions to and who not. The way people process information often determines success or failure in any job assignment or completion of a task. Some very good people fail, or as bad, become totally frustrated, because they are assigned to positions for which their style is unsuited. It's like putting someone who has to have windows and an expansive area to feel good in a small, confined, basement office! I have often thought that one of the reasons The Peter Principle stays alive and well is that we slot people into assignments and tasks for which they have little or no interest, and they slowly become dis-motivated, and then, poor performers. This Profile will allow you to make better decisions, to put the right people in the right positions, and to develop teams of people whose styles are appropriate to the missions at hand.

The fourth and fifth advantages you will gain by using and being aware of the Profile and its distinctive styles go hand-in-hand. Good supervisors know how to **Praise** correctly and how to **Punish** or discipline effectively. Ironically, people often distrust praise. When they receive praise, which is rarely, they tend to be suspicious of it, seeing it as a ploy of manipulation. The reason people feel uneasy with praise is that it is often couched in language that does not "hit home" with the recipient, it is off the mark because it does not speak to the style of the receiver. You will learn how to praise effectively, using the language of the subject, so the deserving employee or officer "hears you," and you will earn credibility in his eyes as you do so. The same holds true for disciplining or punishing a subordinate. If you do not use language appropriate to his or her style, your words will not have the intended effect. The person you are addressing will think you do not know what you are talking about. If you speak to all your troops the same way, you will fail. Some will hear you and others will not. You need to speak to the style of each to be truly effective.

Once you know your style and the styles of those with whom you work, you will be able to **tactically flex** your own style as you move from one person to another. You do not have to like all the people with whom you work, but you do have to be capable of drawing the best from each. Using your new knowledge, you will be less frustrated at differing styles because you will know how to modify your style to adjust appropriately to the styles of others. And, make a note here! It is your responsibility to make the adjustments, not the subordinate! Too many supervisors think their people should adjust to their style. Wrong! It is your job to see that you get through, that you relate to your people. As the "super-sighted one," you must take this as a given. Too many supervisors rely on the "cult of personality" or "the weight of authority" to govern. Wrong. The good supervisor takes as his mission the duty to relate effectively with those below and those above; the bad supervisor demands people adjust to him, and this is destructive and ineffective.

### Communication Profile

The following survey is designed to assist you in identifying and describing the underlying strengths you use in your relationships with other people. You are presented with a number of self-descriptive statements, each of which is followed by four different endings. You are to indicate the order in which you feel each ending is characteristic of yourself. This test has been reproduced on pages 181-185.

In the space provided by each response, fill in the numbers

4   for **most** like you,      3   for **next most** like you,
2   for **less like you**, and   1   for **least like you**.

Fill in **all** blanks for each question, and each question will have 4, 3, 2, or 1. Leave *nothing blank* and do not repeat any number.

**NOTE:**   Answer these questions quickly and naturally. Answer them as you see yourself. Too much thought is **No Good!** Be **Honest!**

1.  **I am likely to impress others as...**

____a.   practical and to the point.
____b.   emotional and somewhat stimulating.
____c.   astute and logical.
____d.   intellectually oriented and somewhat complex.

2.  **In the way I work on projects, I may ...**

____a.   want it to be stimulating and involve lively interaction with others.
____b.   concentrate to make sure the project is systematically or logically developed.
____c.   want to be sure the project has a tangible "pay off" that will justify spending my time and energy on it.
____d.   be most concerned as to whether the project "breaks ground" for advanced knowledge.

3.  **In communicating with others, I may...**

____a.   express unintended boredom with talk that is too detailed.
____b.   convey impatience with those who express ideas that are not thought through.
____c.   show little interest in thoughts and ideas that show little or no originality.
____d.   tend to ignore those who talk about "long range implicators" and direct my attention to what needs to be done right now.

4.  **When confronted by others with a different point of view, I usually make progress by...**

____a.   getting at least one or two specific commitments on which we can "build" later.
____b.   trying to place myself in "the shoes of others."

_____c.   keeping my composure and helping others to see things simply and logically.

_____d.   relying on my basic ability to conceptualize and pull ideas together.

5.  **In terms of time, I probably concentrate most on...**

_____a.   whether what I am doing or planning to do is going to hurt or disturb others.

_____b.   making sure that any actions I take are consistent and part of a systematic progression.

_____c.   my immediate actions and involvements, and whether they make sense today.

_____d.   significant long-range actions I plan to take and how they relate to my life's direction.

6.  **In reaction to individuals whom I meet socially, I am likely to consider...**

_____a.   they contribute ideas and challenges.

_____b.   they seem thoughtful and reflective.

_____c.   they are interesting and fun to be with.

_____d.   they know what they are doing and can get things done.

7.  **I feel satisfied with myself when I...**

_____a.   get more things accomplished than I planned.

_____b.   comprehend the underlying feelings of others and react in a helpful way.

_____c.   solve a problem by using a logical or systematic method.

_____d.   develop new thoughts or ideas, which can be related.

8.  **I find it easy to be convincing when I am...**

_____a.   in touch with my own feelings and those of others.

_____b.   logical, patient and forbearing.

_____c.   down to earth and to the point.

_____d.   intellectually on top of things and take all relevant factors into account.

9.  **I enjoy it when others see me as...**

_____a.   intellectually gifted and having vision.
_____b.   an individual who knows where he is going and has the ability to get there.
_____c.   creative and stimulating.
_____d.   a dependable individual who gets things done and always "comes through."

10. **When circumstances prevent me from doing what I want, I find it useful to...**

_____a.   review any deficiencies or "soft spots" in my approach and modify accordingly.
_____b.   review all that has happened and develop a new hypothesis or model for action.
_____c.   keep in mind the basics, pinpoint the key obstacle(s), and modify my game plan to take these into account.
_____d.   analyze the motivation of others and develop a new "feel" for the situation.

11. **Sometimes I suspect I may come across to others as being...**

_____a.   too emotional or too intense.
_____b.   almost too controlled or perhaps too logical.
_____c.   too concerned with specifics and matters related to "the how to."
_____d.   overly wrapped up in ideas and somewhat hard "to read."

12. **When I write business correspondence to someone I do not know, I usually try to ...**

_____a.   clarify the background reasons for the contact and relate this to my purpose in writing.
_____b.   highlight in plain language what I want, need, or expect of the other.
_____c.   show how my main points fit into a broader perspective.
_____d.   convey at least some information about my style and myself.

13. In speaking before groups with whom I have little regular contact, I like to leave the impression of being...

_____a.    a systematic thinker who can analyze the kind of problems the particular group is concerned about.

_____b.    a broad-gauge thinker capable of making some innovative contribution.

_____c.    a practical and resourceful person who could help the group define its concerns and who can assist in solving its problems.

_____d.    lively and impactful person who was clearly "in touch" with their mood and needs.

14. In tense meetings with others, I may occasionally...

_____a.    let "my hair down" too freely, expressing feelings which might have been better left unsaid.

_____b.    be overly cautious and avoid some contacts which might have proved rewarding.

_____c.    miss the "forest for the trees," become so concerned with a given facet of a person that I fail to see other, less obvious important characteristics.

_____d.    be swayed by others who are gifted but perhaps lacking direction.

15. If I am not careful, others may at times feel that I am...

_____a.    highly unemotional and inclined toward being impersonal or detached.

_____b.    plodding, superficial, or self-centered.

_____c.    somewhat snobbish, intellectual superior or condescending.

_____d.    moody, excitable, or unpredictable.

16. When "the chips are down," I feel it is preferable to...

_____a.    stick to a systematic approach that has proven effective before, even though by taking more risks I might win a few more victories.

_____b.    be respected as original even if it costs me something in the short run.

_____c.    concentrate on getting what I want accomplished right now even if such an approach lacks dramatic impact.

_____d.    be spontaneous and say what I really think.

## 17. When others pressure me I am...

_____a.    overly emotional, impulsive, or apt to get "carried away" by my feelings.

_____b.    too inclined toward being analytical and critical of them.

_____c.    too concerned with proving myself with immediate action.

_____d.    inclined to step back into my own world of thoughts.

## 18. In considering my approach to difficult situations, it is possible that I become overly-involved...

_____a.    in a battle of wits and problem solving, even for their own sake.

_____b.    in the immediate here and now, getting and doing as I wish.

_____c.    in the world of concepts, values, and ideas.

_____d.    about the feelings of others.

## Scoring and Evaluation

Fill in the following chart. There are 18 responses. To the right of each, there are four blanks identified by letters. These represent your responses for each question. Fill in the blanks with the number you put for each letter. Note that the letters are in mixed order, so be careful. When you have completed the first 9, total each column and put the total on the line provided. Reading across, these should add up to 90. Do the same for the last nine. These, too, should add up to 90 reading across.

| RESPONSE | EXP | AN | AM | D |
|----------|-----|----|----|----|
| 1. | d. _____ | c._____ | b. _____ | a. _____ |
| 2. | d. _____ | b. _____ | a. _____ | c. _____ |
| 3. | a. _____ | b. _____ | c. _____ | d. _____ |
| 4. | d. _____ | c. _____ | b. _____ | a. _____ |
| 5. | d. _____ | b._____ | a. _____ | c. _____ |
| 6. | a. _____ | b. _____ | c. _____ | d. _____ |
| 7. | d. _____ | c. _____ | b. _____ | a. _____ |
| 8. | d. _____ | b. _____ | a. _____ | c. _____ |
| 9. | a. _____ | b. _____ | c. _____ | d. _____ |
|  | _____ | _____ | _____ | _____ = 90 |

Top Score

| 10. | b. _____ | a. _____ | d. _____ | c. _____ |
|-----|-----|----|----|----|
| 11. | d. _____ | b. _____ | a. _____ | c. _____ |
| 12. | c. _____ | a. _____ | d. _____ | b. _____ |
| 13. | b. _____ | a. _____ | d. _____ | c. _____ |
| 14. | d. _____ | b. _____ | a. _____ | c. _____ |
| 15. | c. _____ | a, _____ | d. _____ | b. _____ |
| 16. | b. _____ | a. _____ | d. _____ | c. _____ |
| 17. | d. _____ | b. _____ | a. _____ | c. _____ |
| 18. | c. _____ | a. _____ | d. _____ | b. _____ |
|  | _____ | _____ | _____ | _____ = 90 |

Bottom score:

**NOTE:** The top scores represent you under favorable conditions; the bottom scores represent you under stress! Be sure both your top sub-score and your sub-score equal 90 from left to right. If they don't, you have a mistake in addition!

There are four distinct styles:

1. DRIVER (D)
2. ANALYTIC (AN)
3. AMIABLE (AM)
4. EXPRESSIVE (EXP).

The next page defines each style in broad terms, and then we will flesh out the definitions. As you look at your two scores, top and bottom, know that the Mean score is 22, and as you compare top and bottom, 4 or more changes in points is significant! Some of you will change drastically under pressure, the bottom scores, and some of you will not. If you are very consistent, top to bottom, you are steady, but hard to read.

Read scores from top to bottom. "Both S" on the next page, both top and bottom scores.

Scoring Indices

EXPRESSIVE:

(Top score) **Low** = Takes everyday as it comes
            **High** = have long-range goals you're working on

(Bottom score) **Low** = Solves problems quickly, "quick fix"
              **High** = Like permanent solutions, very creative

ANALYTIC:      (Both Scores)
    **Low** = Not a detail person
    **High** = Is good at and enjoys details, processing info
        **Low to High** = Very effective under stress
        **High to Low** = More emotional under stress

AMIABLE:      (Both Scores)
    **Low** = Very private person, doesn't need others

**High** = Very people-oriented

**Low to High** = under pressure, seeks input from others, concerned for others

**High to Low** = Withdraws to make decisions; needs time alone

DRIVER:     (Both Scores)

**Low** = usually more physical than mental

**High** = High energy level; task oriented. High Achiever

**Low to High** = Comfortable with stress; will usually procrastinate; more productive under pressure/stress

**High to Low** = Likes order, likes to be in charge

These general descriptions will give you an idea of the differences in the four styles. Effective leaders know their own styles of processing information so they can more readily flex and match their styles to others with whom they interact. Make a note! **Each style can be an effective style for leadership**. One is not better than another. All are equal in potential leadership ability. The old view, wrong as wrong can be, was that only the hard-nosed, driving CEO could lead departments and companies. We now know this it not true. Each style is as good as the other. Each style has its strengths and its potential weakness. All styles should be represented at the top of any organization so there will be a balance of thrust and focus.

Let's flesh these styles out a bit for you.

The **DRIVER** is a high energy, bottom-line type of personality. Task oriented above all, and forceful and energetic in completing such tasks, the Driver tends to move in a straight line. He is high on telling people what to do, and rarely shows a lot of outward emotion. He is an "I" person, not a "We" person, and he likes to be the leader. He is likely to become impatient with details; he wants answers and solutions, not a lot of discussion. Every style has something it must learn to be more effective, and the Driver clearly needs to learn how to "slow down" and "listen" to others! He or she is a hard-driving, forceful personality, one to be reckoned with, and like a rhino, tends to move at high speed, straight ahead, sometimes at the discomfort of others!

The ANALYTIC, by contrast, tends to be interested in the details and the process of an operation. Analytics like to move cautiously through a problem, considering all angles and permeations. They do not like to be rushed; they trust data and reason, and they like time to think and rethink their course of action. They tend to be precise, information oriented people. Even their hobbies are suggestive of care and detail: chess, tinkering with motors, model airplane building, crossword puzzles, and the like. Like the Driver, they show little outward emotion, but unlike the Driver, they tend to ASK people to do things rather than tell them. They may irritate the quick-moving Driver, but they are excellent people to "watch the back" of the Driver who is likely to jump over the details to get to the goal. This style needs to learn to decide and act! They can become so involved in the details and the processes that they are slow coming to decisions. They like detail and they are good it! Sometimes, too good! But they work hard to be accurate and, make a note, when their work is ignored or treated lightly, they can become deadly enemies!

The AMIABLE is a people person, first and foremost. The Amiable thinks in terms of "We" not "I" and values and evaluates policies and procedures according to their impact on others. Team oriented, the Amiable is concerned for the feelings of others and is empathetic, always attempting to see through the eyes of others. Amiable Bosses will inquire about the personal life of their subordinates because they care, not because they are nosey. Getting to know those with whom they work is important to them, so the time they might spend chatting with a colleague at the water fountain is not wasted time. They have in the past been maligned for being "touchy-feely" types with no backbone to lead others, but we now know this is not true. Indeed, if upper management legislates policies or procedures that are harmful to the well-being of the employees, Amiables will fight to change them. Any Boss, who habitually ignores his people's welfare, makes an enemy of the Amiable. To show you how much the Amiable cares about the team and the organization, when attacked personally by a superior, the Amiable more often than not will defer for the sake of the group. He or she will not make a "scene" that might jeopardize the overall well-being of the team. The Amiable puts the group ahead of himself. Like the Analytic, the Amiable is high on asking people to cooperate, but unlike the

Analytic, is the Amiable high on emotion as well. He or she will wear his "heart on his sleeve." Emotion is good, true, and trustworthy for the Amiable.

A special note on the amiable personality. In the years that I have used this Profile with departments large and small across the United States, rarely have I found an Amiable represented among the top echelon people. This is a holdover from the older, traditional view that Amiables are too "mushy" or weak to lead, an old concept we now know to be false. In the larger departments, the top people tend to be Drivers, Analytics, or the combinations Driver-Analytic or Analytic-Drivers. Often, in the larger departments, the major complaint from the troops is they feel the Bosses have forgotten where they came from, forgotten the people who do the work. If you happened to be one of these Driver-Analytic combinations, follow this advice: **seek out an Amiable**, at whatever level he or she may be found, and pass your ideas on to them for evaluation. These people will give you feedback you cannot get from anyone else. They will evaluate your proposals in terms of the human impact, at work and even at home. A department or organization becomes a much more human place to live and work when Amiables have a say in what is done.

Finally, the **EXPRESSIVE,** the actor of the group, possessing high energy and a love for the "role" or the "act." The Expressive likes to be dramatic, above all else. He puts **himself** into everything he does. Like the Driver, the Expressive is high on Telling people what to do and high on "I." Where the Driver may show little or no emotion, and value such, Expressives believe in wearing their hearts on their sleeves, indeed, they insist on it! They tend to decorate their actions as they decorate their offices. Style and élan are important to them; they hate being thought boring and "average," and they will go to great lengths to make sure they are never seen in these lights. It is "showtime" all the time to the Expressive! They are easily frustrated by details and routine, often preferring to create their own rhythms and ways of doing things. Not easily team players, they enjoy the spotlight and the drama of being "different." Like the Driver, they need to learn how to "slow down" and listen to others. Because they are so focused on doing whatever they do with 'style,' they are often thought to be egotistic. More often than not it's a style difference, not a matter of egoism.

To appreciate fully the connections and relationships of these styles to one another, consult the box diagram below, where you see all four styles and how they relate one to another.

**Low Emotion**

| Analytic | Driver |
|----------|--------|
| Amiable | Expressive |

**High Ask** (left) **High Tell** (right)

**High Emotion**

This box diagram, with the four quadrants, shows the relationship of the four styles, one to another. Notice that the Driver and the Analytic share the Low Emotion trait, and the Amiable and the Expressive share the trait of High Emotion. The Driver and the Expressive are alike in that they both are high on Tell as a style of dealing with people, where the Analytic and the Amiable like to Ask people for cooperation. What is really interesting is the cross quadrant connections: Expressive to Analytic and Driver to Amiable. These cross quadrant styles tend to be naturally antithetical to one another. The style of each raises hackles with the other. For example, the Driver looks at an Amiable and tends to think, "weak, mushy, too touchy-feely." The Amiable looks at the Driver and sees a hard line, often harsh, insensitive personality, capable of hurting others in his drive to success. The Expressive looks at the Analytic and thinks, "Boring! Too detailed, too slow, too cautious, just frustrating to be around. And the Analytic looks at the Expressive and sees too much flash, much like a snake oil salesman, too egotistic and careless! A loose cannon!

To flex your style effectively, you will first have to know what style the other has and then be capable of moving around the quadrants, constantly modifying your style as you go. How can you know the other's style? Ideally, you will give the Profile questionnaire to your troops. But often you will have to deal with people where this ideal condition cannot be met. So, **listen** to how the other talks and by doing so become clued in. If you hear words such as "analyze, research, think over, use logic, what are the facts," you know you are facing an Analytic. If you happen to be an Expressive, begin to use more cautious, analytical type language as you explain what you want, **otherwise you will not be heard, literally**! Because the Expressive is so different from the Analytical in his presentation style, the Analytic will have a hard time paying attention to the points being made for he will be more put off by the contrary style. You are *not* being phony or insincere when you flex, only tactically smart. If you put your ideas and substance before your ego, you will modify your entire approach to have an honest hearing and have a positive impact. If you are talking with an Amiable, and hoping to get their compliance, choose words from their "world of values," words like "team, group, we," and show how your ideas are good for people! If, for example, you are a Driver, and you talk only about the bottom line, the goal, you will not influence the Amiable. He has to see your ideas in an "amiable light" for him to get onboard.

Listening is not the only way to recognize a person's habitual processing style. If you are in another's office, look around! What do you see that might clue you as to their style? If you see, for example, a lot of family pictures and group pictures, you might guess the person is an Amiable, and begin by asking about the family or the groups you see. Such an approach makes an Amiable more comfortable with you. Don't start with data, you Analytics, or with the task at hand, you Drivers, or you will find resistance. Finding common ground creates rapport, and a person's style is your first clue. Perhaps it's the way a person dresses, or the way he or she decorates the office, home, or car. Look and listen, and it won't take you long to make an educated guess as to someone's predominant style! Watch the face, a great book for style. Quizzical looks, penetrating stares, a raised eyebrow—all characteristics of the Analytical. Knowing what you know now, you can fill in the blanks for the other styles.

To complicate matters just a bit more, many of us have a foot in two quadrants, two styles, one more dominant than the other, usually. Many of the top commanders I taught at LAPD and LASO were Driver-Analytics. Indeed, in my own experience, I have found this to be a dominant hybrid style in police work, and in corporate America. Such people might also be Analytic-Drivers, depending on the Profile. I, myself, am an Expressive-Driver. If you have ever seen me teach you know I jump around and get into people's faces, trying to be as dynamic as I can (the Expressive me) to get the point across, (the Driver in me)! As you look at your top and bottom scores, you may well note that your style **changes** under stress. You may be a Driver who, under stressful conditions, becomes an Analytic, perhaps because you know you have to get the details right to be successful. Or you may be primarily an Analytic who changes to Driver because you know all your work is for naught if you don't complete the task at hand. There are Analytic-Amiables, and Amiable-Analytics; Amiable-Expressives and Expressive-Amiables, and Expressive-Drivers, Driver-Expressives. Interesting to look at your scores and see how you change as conditions change.

Rarely will you find the **cross-quadrants** paired, but it happens. I have found that the best Sergeants on the streets are often Driver-Amiables or Amiable-Drivers! Perhaps this anomaly happens because the good Sergeant knows he has to relate well to people to be successful, so he flexes his styles consistently the Amiable way. Your present job assignment can, and does, influence your scores, particularly the Top score. In business I have found that such people who are Drivers become more Amiable under stress because they know that to be successful they must seek the input of their people to get the job done. One drawback to the cross-quadrant hybrid may be that when people first meet you and begin working for you they will find you confusing, perhaps even contradictory. Over time, they will learn to trust your opposite style, but it may take time.

Knowing the styles can make all the difference in helping you assess how you want to handle people, one on one or in a group. For example, let's say you are a Chief who has to go before the City Council to ask for more funds for your department's salaries. A major part of your research should include analyzing the Council, individually and as a group. Let's say you find that the majority of people are Analytics, an Accountant, a Banker, and basically numbers people. How will you begin your presentation? With your request? Your ideas? NO, you will come armed with charts and graphs showing in painstaking detail how your department compares with others of similar size. Show the data, the proof that a raise for your people is needed. Take your time, be prepared to answer numerous questions, and have the data to support any assertions you intend to make. You can be sure the meeting will run on the longish side, and be prepared to come back again, perhaps even suggest the Council should take time to look over the material you have brought! Such people have to be shown in detail that a raise for the troops is necessary. Be also prepared to show the monies are readily available...do your research!

Such an approach for a Council predominantly Drivers and Expressives would be a severe error! The Driver and the Expressive value time, they want to know NOW, they want the quick, down and dirty approach. Do not start with charts and graphs! Start with your bottom line, talk about morale and community service, and show that better troops in the field will make the City (and of course the Council) look good! The bottom-line is for the Drivers is "What needs to be done" and the appeal to looking good is the bottom line for the Expressives. Be prepared to hand some data and proof over to the Council. They will have an Analytic look over your stuff, but they will not, themselves, take the time at the meeting. Time is money! Be prepared to be short, direct, and to the point! AND "interesting!" Don't bore Expressives or Drivers, the former because he will think you are dull and insipid, and the latter because he has better ways to spend his time!

To see if you really get the differences, pretend you are a life insurance salesman and you have made appointments at four homes, each home houses a different style. You have been allotted an hour of time. Think how you would handle each visit. You know in the Analytic's home, you will take the whole hour; you will spread out all your printed material and charts that demonstrate why your policy is a good one and how it is better than your competitor's. You will be prepared to answer many questions, and you will probably want to emphasize that your policy is the most thorough and solid one. You will also perhaps suggest that the Analytic take some time to consider the materials you have brought. Calendar another appointment to make the sale. Your hour will most probably be spent in the study or den.

With the Driver, you will want to be brief, precise, and clear as to the benefits of your policy. Since time is everything to the Driver, take little of it. Show the Driver it's the best "bang for his dollar" and get out. Bring supporting literature with you, but do not go over it with him; he or she will find someone else to do that. You will be fortunate to make it as far as the living room. The Driver will either sign immediately, once he is assured he has the best policy, or he will tell you when he will. Do not press the Driver to act. Clearly put forth your policy's strengths and he will make a quick decision. The same efficient process must be taken with the Expressive, with one crucial difference: make the Expressive feel good about his making the choice. Make him see that by purchasing life insurance for his family he is the "hero," the provider, the watchdog. It is his one great unselfish act! Do not bore either with details or data. Show each how they will benefit from going with your policy.

The Amiable is wholly different. A good place for the meeting might well be the kitchen, where you will sit and have coffee and chat about his or her family, and your family. Of your allotted hour, perhaps 40 minutes or more will be learning about each other. Do not be in a hurry to get to the policy. The Amiable must come to trust you before he or she will buy. When you do pitch your policy, emphasize its benefit to the family, the kids and their kids. The Amiable must feel good about signing on and he must see the benefits to his entire family. He may want you to return for a second visit before signing, if only to meet his wife and kids who were out shopping at the time. IF he doesn't mention it, perhaps you should!

You should now see that trying to sell the same policy the same way to four different families will not succeed, except perhaps with one. Selling a life insurance policy is not much different than selling an idea, so be alert to the styles and vary accordingly.

If you think about it, trying to perceive others' style and flexing accordingly can be a fun and interesting exercise. When we suggested earlier that a good supervisor must be the ultimate Chameleon you can now see the kind of changes you can make that will help you blend and flex with the audiences you encounter. Subtle linguistic changes, physical changes, and modifications of **how you present**, and how you decide what to present first and what later, is how you "Chameleon Up" to the situation. Failure to make these changes means failure at all levels.

Let's take a few scores and see what we can make of them. This will help you analyze your own style and those of your subordinates. Remember, all styles are equally capable of great leadership. There is no better or worse. Take these scores:

| EXP | AN | AM | DRIVER |
|-----|-----|-----|--------|
| 21 | 23 | 13 | 33 |
| 22 | 19 | 26 | 23 |

Recall that 22 is the Mean score, and 4 or more point difference between top and bottom score is significant. This person is clearly a Driver under normal conditions (33). Note the low Amiable score (13) that suggests this person does not need, or consult people. It doesn't mean he doesn't "like" people; just that he doesn't work through and with people under normal conditions. He prefers to do it himself. Not so under stress, the bottom score. Note here that under stress this person turns to people (26) and works through people to accomplish the tasks. Also note the 19 under Analytic, a four point fall from the top score of 23, suggesting that under pressure this person becomes less concerned for details, perhaps even careless with them. You can see the importance of knowing—being Consciously Competent—regarding the shifts you take as conditions change. Were these your scores, you would know that, when under stress, you would want to remind yourself to pay additional attention to details, or have someone else check you as you go. Perhaps, too, since you know you rely on people under stress, you may want to try to involve more people in your work under favorable, less stressful conditions.

What if you were reading a score of one of your subordinates that was just the reverse of the one above? What would you say?

| EXP | AN | AM | DRIVER |
|-----|-----|-----|--------|
| 22 | 19 | 26 | 23 |
| 21 | 23 | 13 | 33 |

You would point out that the person is an Amiable, people-centered, most of the time, and a bit uninterested in details, paperwork, and data, but under pressure he turns into a Driver, and becomes more attentive to details and process. Notice that under stress this person prefers to jump in and take over the tasks, not needing people to help him work. The strength of this shift, of course, is that the person seems to take a leadership role and works independently of others, paying more attention to details and the goal. The danger might be that the people he works with will feel he ignores their input and isn't a team player at all. Once your subordinate is aware of this potential shift, he or she can make an additional effort to involve others or at least keep them informed so they do not feel left out.

Often in class when I do these exercises, some, when they receive their readings, say, "That's not me!" Usually those in the class that know the individual say, "Oh yes it is!" Remember, **you** put the numbers down! You may not realize just how you do process, but others will tell you those numbers are truly you! Interesting!

Since you will have to analyze your own score, let me help you by analyzing mine first. Here are my scores. What do you make of these?

| EXP | AN | AM | DRIVER |
|-----|-----|-----|--------|
| 30  | 17  | 18  | 25     |
| 24  | 16  | 26  | 24     |

As you can see, I am an Expressive Driver, and not people or detail oriented. But under pressure, I even out, becoming an Amiable, with equal stress on Expressive and Driver. I tend to want to work through and with people under difficult conditions, and in both cases, I have to watch the details! Not surprising, is it, that I picked as my Vice President an Analytic? I know my potential weakness is details and process, so years ago I brought Mr. Lee Fjelstad on to "watch my back" and ensure we do things in a detailed, analytic manner. Thank goodness, my wife is also partly an Analytic, although she is strongest in the Driver category.

My co-author, Greg, is an Amiable Expressive.

This leads me to mention other interesting uses for this Profile. Use it with your family! Allow your wife or husband to take this Profile, then sit and discuss what you see. Perhaps you will discover why you get along so well, or understand why you have areas of hot conflict! In either case you will learn a great deal about your "other half" and the relationship between you. Above the age of 18 or so, your children can usefully respond to this Profile as well, and again the knowledge you gain can be wonderfully useful.

It is crucial you consider using your knowledge of the styles whenever you intend to develop a Team within your department. Ideally, a team should consist of one of each of the styles, so that all the bases are covered. Depending on the mission, however, you might want more of one type than another. In assigning jobs, consider the person's Profile. Although all styles **can** do what you assign them, and most will endeavor to do the best they can, whenever it is possible, try to put people into jobs and positions that will harmonize with their style. For example, were you to assign me a task working computers, in a windowless room, for a long period of time, it would put me under terrific stress! As An Expressive Driver, I need room and activity! Sitting long hours, working on detailed work, would wear on me and gradually lower my morale. Put an Analytic there instead! Who might best be put to work in schools, as a Community Officer, working with kids? Probably an Amiable. Perhaps an Expressive, but an Analytic or Driver might chaff at such "people" work. It is not always possible, of course, to match the style with the job, but whenever possible, it is helpful, both to the department and to the assigned officer.

You will see when we get to the chapters on Praise and Punishment how important the styles are in doing both well. For now, feel free to use the questionnaire in the back of the book to copy and give to your subordinates and peers. Remember when dealing with your superiors you should attempt to define their styles and modify your approach accordingly. Across the board, knowing another's style markedly enhances your ability to communicate effectively and successfully.

## CHAPTER EIGHT

# MOTIVATION AND REASSURANCE

The visionary leader knows that to be effective, he must follow the primary principle of supervision, which is to **Direct** others rather than try to **Control** them. Like the director of a play, the best leader and supervisor trains his people, runs them through exercises, and prepares them for the tasks at hand. Then, like the director, the best leader and supervisor allows his people to play out their roles to the fullest extent of their cultivated capabilities. In a play, if the play is successful, the players receive the credit; if the play is a flop, the director takes the heat. So, too, should it be in management and supervision. You want to use your wisdom, not the force of authority, to see your people and organization successful.

One tool critical to success lies in you knowing the unique personality styles we have presented and discussed, then using these effectively to accomplish the organizational mission. On a daily basis, much of your effort as a supervisor must be directed in **motivating** your people properly. To do this well, you must first know and use the Principle of Motivation I have developed at the Verbal Judo Institute. There are hundreds of ways to motivate people, some good and some truly awful. As a supervisor you may be relying on your own methods now but the most effective way rests on but one bottom-line principle: **"Raise the Expectations of Others!"** Whatever it is you do, your actions must raise a subordinate or employee's expectations of himself so that he or she can accomplish more than their current self-assessment gives them credit for. Once people believe they can do more and are properly encouraged, trained, and given the responsibility to do so, they will often surprise themselves and you! Robert Browning, the English poet, once said, "A man's reach must exceed his grasp." As a supervisor, your responsibility is to inculcate a new belief system into your people. **Raising Expectations** is not forcing your expectations on others or holding them accountable to the same. Rather, it is planting the correct motivational seed in the employee's mind that he is capable of much more than he now believes. You want to lift your people up, and help them build their personalities beyond the current threshold they've created for themselves. You want to take them from where they are to where you know they are capable of going.

For example, when my son Taylor was in school, he came home one day with a report card that had four "A's" and one "F." He handed it to me with some apprehension. I looked at, and instinctively wanted to say, "Hey, what's this 'F'?" I was ready to pounce on him, but something made me stop. Instead of lambasting him, I said, "Gosh, Taylor, I never got four 'As' at this grade level...you even got one in Math! Wow!" I handed the card back to him and started to walk away. He said, "Hey, Dad, didn't you miss something?" I replied, "Oh, you mean the 'F'?"

"Yeah, the 'F,'" he said.

I replied, "It occurs to me Taylor that if you can get four 'A's' you must have meant to get that 'F.' He brightened as he said, "Yeah, Dad, I don't like the teacher so I purposely didn't work for him."

I said, "Interesting, but you know, I have studied power for years, and I have had teachers I didn't like, too. I thought about them just the way you do. But it occurred to me one day that I was playing into their hands by not working. That allowed them to give me the 'F' and they probably enjoyed being able to do so. I decided that if I didn't like a teacher, perhaps the most powerful thing I could do was to make him give me a good grade! If I could make him give me an 'A' or 'B' and they didn't like me, I won a battle! They had to do it! That's power in my book."

Taylor didn't say much, but the next report card he showed me demonstrated I'd properly motivated him. "Look at the grade from Mr. X, Dad. I made him give me that 'B'!"

Had I jumped on him for the initial "F," I would have reinforced his feelings of failure, and I would have made my expectations dominant and not necessarily successful over the long run. Instead I motivated him to raise his own expectations *of himself* and confirmed for him that he had the power to get whatever grade he chose to. He took his own power back, and he was prouder of that "B" than of any of the other grades he got that year!

In Baghdad, while managing a high-risk security detail under the most violent and stressful of circumstances and conditions, my co-author did the same. One particularly competent and street-wise individual on his detail began to show a talent for organization. Greg watched him carefully, assigned him some minor organizational tasks, then moved him from "running and gunning" to managing the daily organizational planning and movement of the team's Client.

After awhile, the young man said he believed that it would be better to work the street detail than to manage the growing multitude of organizational challenges and tasks at hand. Greg showed him by careful, thoughtful discussion, how truly good this individual was in an area of expertise the Team needed to be successful and to stay alive. The young man went on to spend over three years in Iraq, working for the best of companies, and always a valued asset whether carrying a gun or helping plan and manage daily operations.

Raising expectations rather than dampening enthusiasm is an important leadership strategy. For example, an employee might come to you with an idea he wants to pursue and you might initially feel he isn't ready for such a task at the moment. The all too often normal response is to launch into all the reasons that come to mind why the employee should move more cautiously, if at all. The employee will leave your office feeling put down and disappointed. Keep in mind if he thought of the idea, he has a desire to pursue it. You want to encourage his desire, perhaps assuring him that you will help in any way you can, and pointing out that although the path may be difficult, you believe he has the "stuff" to make it happen. If he is not ready at the moment, you, as a quality supervisor, need to not only explain why perhaps the idea requires more time to be developed, but offer also to provide the employee with the tools to successfully bring the idea, or plan, or project to fruition! This is quality motivation and sound employee care taking.

It is also quality leadership.

As you think about how to raise the personal expectations of your people, remember their personality styles. Always frame your discussion **in the language and the context of the other party**. When talking with an Analytic that may have failed to measure up, point out that you are surprised his work was so imprecise given his usual high level of detailed expertise. The Analytic, who prides himself on details and accuracy, will respond to your commentary positively because he inherently cares about such precision **and** he will appreciate your knowing something about him that he believes is important to his self and work image. With an Amiable, show that whatever the person failed to do correctly could harm the team as a whole and make it more difficult for the people around him to succeed. In both cases you will "hit home" with your comments and each will strive to do better because success is important to both personality types. It is almost impossible to motivate someone concerning things they do not care about so the trick is to find the right connection that shows the employee why you, as his supervisor, knows he instinctively cares and wants to be successful. This is where you have to use your wisdom, your super-vision, if you will, to broaden his perspective.

In discussing a situation with a Driver, for example, if you can show that what he did resulted in a failure to reach the goal, he will want to make another and better attempt at the job. With the Expressive, point out that what he did put him in a bad light with others, and he normally has a better image in the department than this last performance. The Expressive is concerned with his image and will respond by wanting to correct his behavior. Help the Expressive see himself as he would like to be seen, and he will respond positively to your recommendations.

The best supervisors see their job as bringing their charges along, helping them succeed and even surpassing what they themselves believed beyond their present capabilities. The good supervisor puts his ego aside and seeks to correctly build up a new and constructive ego in his people. He refrains from putting people down because he knows that put-downs only weaken their spirit. We have worked with far too many supervisors who felt they had to be one step ahead of their people, felt they had to put others down so everyone remembered, at a minimum, *who the boss is*. These are weak supervisors and, often, weak people. Such a learning curve, as we recommend, teaches employees that such strategies, tactics and techniques are not only normal, they are expected! Is it any wonder that the sadly traditional manner of creating managers and supervisors has led us down the miserable path to where we are today? Great leaders and supervisors grow in strength and influence as their people grow in maturity and capability.

Above all, you must be **consistent** and **disciplined** in your approach. You cannot be encouraging and uplifting one day, and negative and discouraging the next! Because people are different, ideally you will have a "plan" for each employee, one that takes into consideration his particular personality style and his expressed goals both personal and professional. Evaluate the progress of each subordinate and constructively challenge each appropriately. Giving people increased responsibility builds their confidence but only if you support the greater responsibility with quality training and the proper tools to get the job done at the next level. You must seek to provide opportunities for your people to be truly successful within their newly challenged capability. This is where your guidance and direction comes into play. Sequence the challenges and tasks according to your assessment of the employee's ability and his or her style. You must constantly monitor and correctly assess his progress. Too big a challenge can discourage; too small can seem insignificant and meaningless. Some will respond better to smaller, more manageable tasks, and others will like the more dramatic jumps. Know your people and assign tasks as appropriate.

In all endeavors, however, always start with what the person does well, and use this built-in confidence level to construct increased confidence. Everyone does something well, or at least better than others, and this should be your starting point. The most crucial principle of learning is what we call **Known to Unknown!** In order to teach people and see them successfully learn from your teaching, you must take them from what they **know** to what they **do not** know. Begin with their strengths, and use those strengths to motivate them to move to a new level, the "unknown", where you want them to be. Bad supervisors, like bad teachers, move from **known to known**, never challenging or motivating their people to do more or to do better. Or they move from **unknown to unknown,** always expecting something from their people but never clarifying what those standards and expectations are. This is in part a power trip, or game, on the part of the poor supervisor or teacher. People who are so supervised or taught never feel challenged or excited. Indeed, they feel they should just coast, doing the minimum, and not upsetting the easygoing, lax pace of the supervisor or office pontiff. People under such systems never know what to expect or how they are being judged or evaluated. Reward and discipline seem arbitrary, even capricious. Standards are never clarified and expectations never clearly set forth. Employees are left to guess what the supervisor wants and oftentimes they are proven wrong.

As a role model, you must dramatize to your people how you want them to be and what you expect them to become. You yourself must be an example of energy and commitment, and you must set your own expectations high and then share them with your people. Remember you are an **Ethical Force**. As people see you strive, so will they strive. Demonstrate in your daily interactions with others that you care about excellence and that you care about them becoming excellent. You must share your vision with your people, and ask for their help in attaining that vision. A real team shares a vision, and as supervisor, you are, and must be, the vision maker! Your energy must draw others to you; others must desire to share in that energy and participate in your vision.

The task is not always easy. Often employees become frustrated in their pursuit of excellence and falter. The good supervisor must then be a master of using the language of **Reassurance** to embolden his people once they begin to weaken. There are many ways to reassure someone, but the Principle of Reassurance is Empathy. **Empathy absorbs tension**! Empathy is an interesting word, a combination of Latin and Greek. "Em" is Latin for "to see through," and "pathy" is Greek for "eye of other." The ability to see as others see is the source of your power as a quality leader and supervisor. It is how you can connect with others, and in turn connect them with you. Empathy means **to understand**, it does not mean to agree or to sympathize with. People need to know you care enough to attempt to understand their positions, even if you do not agree with them, and they also need to believe that you care enough to share your vision with them.

The best supervisors never forget where they came from, that they themselves were once troops or frontline workers. To remember what it was like to be where your people are now is a great source of strength for you, so use it! This is again where the "Hook-Down" theory will help you stay "in touch" with your people. Being able to think like your people is truly a gift. A salesman, who forgets what it is like to buy, sells poorly. I recently went house hunting with a realtor who showed all the signs of "burn-out." The realtor wanted the sale, and never once showed empathy for how hard it was for my wife Pam and I to jump in and out of the car, with a five-month-old baby, to preview yet another house, and worse, when we finally settled on a house, he showed no empathy for our agonizing about how we could finance that house! At that point, when we were under pressure and tension, the realtor should have helped us think through our quandary. Indeed, he should have served us by **thinking for us as we might have thought for ourselves under better conditions**! Such "service" is the service provided by police officers when they deal with domestic disputes and the like, and so, too, is the service supervisors must be prepared to offer their charges when they find themselves under pressure. Without empathy, this category of quality service is impossible!

Reassurance begins and ends with seeing through the eye of the other. To motivate and challenge you must first **see as your people see**. One of the greatest motivators is what we will later call **The Personal Appeal**. People naturally want to do what is in their best interests. Don't you? If you strive to see from another's point of view, you will ultimately discover what lies in his best interest because you will learn what he sees as being his best interest! Use that, his own positive selfishness, to move him to higher levels of achievement. Often you will have to persuade others to do what you want them to do by first showing them that what you want them to do is good for them. One of the best ways to convince others that you do understand is to use their personal needs to ignite their desire to do more and do it better! If you begin and end with what you alone want, you are doomed to failure in most cases. The empathetic supervisor, by contrast, begins with what he perceives his people wants or needs, and then uses these perceived needs and desires to motivate his people to be where he wants them to be. People need to see their upward journey at work and at home as their own, and this is the secret of successful motivation as utilized by a quality leader, supervisor, or manager.

## CHAPTER NINE

# THE ART OF PRAISE

O nce you reconstruct your belief that the Principle of
Motivation is to raise the expectations of your people *of
themselves* and once you believe that Empathy is the
secret for staying in touch with your people, you are ready to
employ the most powerful supervision tool of all, **Praise.** Indeed,
praise both reaffirms and reassures people that what they are
doing is right and good and in line with the organization's
practices, goals, and objectives. Everyone desires and indeed
needs praise, though few of us receive it often enough and
properly. By definition, the police world, for example is filled with
coming into contact and correcting error. Officers on the streets
are challenged to confront negative behavior and then act on it.
Cops advise, warn, cite, and arrest people for alleged wrong behavior and actions. It is no surprise, then, that when police
officers are elevated to positions of leadership and supervision
they naturally seek to maintain their now finely tuned fault-
detecting instincts. In non-law enforcement fields and professions
the same holds true but for different reasons. Far too many
supervisors are, as employees and subordinates, trained in the
workplace to distrust their fellow employees and indeed their
supervisors. Suspicion and skepticism is a way of life in the
American work environment. This negative, destructive pattern
continues unabated and, with promotion, the cycle goes on.

With promotion, your view as a new supervisor or manager
may change dramatically even while perpetuating the negative
focus you learned while an hourly wage earner. Where before you
were one of "the guys," you are now in charge of the guys. Where
before, you, too, chaffed at shortsighted and inept supervision,
now you are that miserable SOB the guys (and gals!) despised.
You will naturally gravitate toward terms like "correction" and
"discipline" rather than **encouragement** and **stimulation**.
Promotion in bad work environments is inherent with this
reverse leadership logic! I once knew a brilliant high school
teacher; one revered by his students for his stress on
independence and free thinking who, once promoted to Principal,
became a nightmare of discipline, order, and punishment! His

view of his world changed dramatically once he was in position to lead and supervise. Yet he never seemed aware of this dramatic change in himself. When I pointed out the differences between his "then and now" behavior, he denied it was true but added that indeed order and conformity were "obviously important" in a school setting! Amazing! Both my co-author and I have seen this phenomenon occur over and over in teaching, business, military and police work. Rarely are the newly promoted aware of their transition to managerial monster. If they admit to being so aware, they often rationalize the change as "necessary and right," given their new status! People seem to have a natural tendency to forget where they came from, to forget how they felt when they were on the front lines, and such blindness to their own pasts creates havoc and disaster for them in the present once the reins of leadership are entrusted to them.

The police leader and supervisor, unlike most other professions, has already developed a negative need for control and order from his days on the street as a patrol officer. When promoted, most supervisors ratchet this negative perspective up a few notches and continue on as before, finding fault and error in the people below him. They identify the wrongdoers they were hired to detect, arrest, and help prosecute with their own subordinates and begin to treat everyone the same...like *crap*. Aiding and abetting this tendency is the prevailing "macho" view that cops should be able to "take it," only wimps and softies require praise and encouragement. I have had many supervisors tell me that their people simply need to "suck it up" and "get with the program." Interesting that this is what cops all too often hear from abusive husbands when investigating domestic violence cases.

Perhaps one reason people suspect praise as a viable and constructive management tool is that when it is given, it often is given improperly, and hence even the people being praised feel uneasy or suspect of the motivation behind what may be very real, heartfelt praise. As a motivator, praise is one of the most powerful tools we can use, but it must be presented correctly.

What do we know about praise? First, it must be **Believable, Credible**, and **Appropriate** to the situation and person. As well, it needs to be **Timely** and if at all possible, **Public**, where others can hear it. Making praise believable and credible is not easy. Have you ever praised someone; only to have them suspect you are "setting them up" for something they won't want to do? Make a note! The fault lies not with them but with your presentation of the praise and encouragement you want to give!

There is a secret to effective praise that we know of and that is **BE SPECIFIC!** General praise is next to worthless because it convinces no one. "Hey, great job" you say to one of your employees, and he thinks, "what's so great about it? I do this all the time. Why is he mentioning it now? What does he really want?" And, remember our Personality Styles? If you frame your praise in words not in synch with his or her personality style, the praise will not hit home with the right impact you as a supervisor desire. The employee or subordinate being praised is unable to correctly translate from how you deliver your commentary to belief that you really know or appreciate his, or her, particular contribution.

Specific praise is powerful and an important form of tactical communication because it accomplishes several important missions, both for you and your subordinate / employee. One, it **Teaches** the person what you really want and respect! I remember being assigned a perimeter watch position on a SWAT operation. I felt a bit left out of the real action but I knew my watch was necessary, just in case one or more of the subjects got away from the team. When the mission went down without a hitch, and the bad guys were all corralled and being taken to jail, my lieutenant came up to me and said, "Hey, George, I really appreciate the care you took out there watching the perimeter. Officer safety is important and you were alert and ready." I felt great! I felt I, too, had contributed, and I knew by his comments that he had **noticed** my being there. By being specific, the lieutenant had proven to me that he indeed did value officer safety and he had been attentive to my work. In the future, whenever he talked about officer safety, I knew he believed in it and rewarded officers for it. His praise sold me on his professional concerns and made them mine even more so.

Specific praise also **Reinforces** employee values and skills. You can be sure that the lieutenant's comments strengthened my own belief in officer safety, teamwork, and in doing whatever I was assigned, well. I began to pride myself on my ability to watch over others, and be the "protector." His praise instilled in me that **conscious** desire to continue to do what I had done before but without much emphasis...I was doing my job. His praise sharpened my own sense of safety and my potential contribution so my job took on greater import and meaning. He raised my expectations of my own future performance!

By pointing out my contribution specifically, the lieutenant also **Stimulated** me to do more in the same arena. Where before I had seen perimeter work as somewhat "out of the action," I now saw it as crucial to the team's work, and I looked for more assignments like that. He stimulated my desire to be part of a team and he had taught me that no job is small or insignificant in a team endeavor. As an Expressive Driver, he had hit home, too, because his praise made me feel good about the way I saw myself in relation to others, one concern of the Expressive, and I had made a contribution to the bottom line, a Driver's concern, officer safety.

Thus, this leader and supervisor earned **credibility**. The word credibility comes from the Latin word "Credo" meaning "belief," and his specific comments made me believe he had noticed me and noticed my work. He was indeed a "seeing eye." The "super-sight" of the supervisor was proven through his correct use of praise.

Being "out there" is important. Remember the Hook-Down theory, but equally important is to **Look** at people, as they operate in the field, and write specifically about the contributions of each. If the sergeants, for example, write their reports focusing specifically on the contributions of the team, the lieutenant can then read those reports and from said reports seek out those he wishes to praise specifically and well. Part of being "out there", of staying on the floor or in the streets with your employees, is developing that "super sight" that looks for the good in your people's work and then takes the time and effort to track them down and deliver the proper praise and encouragement. One thing to consider as you read this chapter is to **Teach** yourself to look for specific good in the work of your people and then to report this work in writing so you or your supervisor can then acknowledge good work. Nothing stimulates front-line employees more than having one of the "Big Dawgs" take the time to search them out and praise the work they are doing!

You need, therefore, to know how to deliver effective praise and you need to teach others, primarily those coming up the promotion ladder behind you, this same management skill.

1.  Look at your employee's work.
2.  Note how you Feel about his work.
3.  Define precisely what he or she did that made you notice the effort and how it contributed to the Whole. This is where you locate and define the specifics!—and
4.  When you deliver the praise, combine your Feeling, ("I am pleased...") with the Specific Action ("about the way you handled X in the field").

When right feeling is combined with correct specifics, people believe you. Generalities miss the mark, specifics hit home!

The **kind of specifics** you mention make all the difference in the world in whether you motivate the employee and if he or she believes you. Recall our Personality Styles. It is possible to praise a group of people, a team for example, and not connect with any one of them, or perhaps, at best, with only one. Let us imagine, for example, that your SWAT team has performed a successful extraction of hostages and you have arrested the bad guys, no lives lost and no one hurt. As you gather to debrief, you, the leader, praise the group for a successful mission, the goal was accomplished, and the bad guys taken down. If you leave it at that, addressing the entire group, you may find your individual team members are less than happy with your comments. Some may even feel you didn't really see the full success at all of the team. Most will privately offer, "same old debrief."

The Analytic member of the team, for example, may have waited in vain for you to praise the careful planning and tactics of the venture that he had been responsible for. The Driver member may be happy with your comments, because the bottom line was accomplished, but the Amiable member may feel you missed the point—everyone worked together in harmony and no one was hurt! The Expressive member may feel you did not fully appreciate his leadership, or perhaps he may feel you missed how good the OP looked from the community point of view.

Whenever possible, praise people according to your prior understanding and study of the personality styles on your team or work group. That way they really hear you and feel you know what you are talking about. People are motivated by praise, yes, but that praise has to be specific and relevant to their processing style. Otherwise they simply do not think you "get it," and often they will be right!

And finally, you will often find yourself having both positive and negative things to say to someone. Thompson's Law, based on thousands of officers and middle managers experiences, goes like this:

> **NEVER PRAISE AND THEN CRITICIZE.**
> **CRITICIZE FIRST, AND THEN END WITH PRAISE!**

The all too natural thing is to praise first, and then criticize on the tail end. This comes across as softening your people up before you hammer them, and this approach leads to resentment and failure. Because people are naturally suspicious of praise to begin with, when they hear it they tend to brace themselves for the negative they believe is coming. They think, "Bend over—here it comes!" Even if you are sincere in your initial praise, many, out of previous poor conditioning and training by inept leaders and supervisors before you, will see it as a slam tactic and shut you out before you can deliver "the good news."

Always mention the negative first, again being specific about what you found lacking, and then end with praise, also being specific. People tend to believe the last thing they hear, and your commentary comes across as balanced if you get the "nuts and bolts" out of the way right up front. Employees so praised leave your presence feeling better about themselves and their performance in the end...and they know everyone can and will seek to do better because you will be helping rather than hindering. Ending with praise also makes it more difficult for someone to feel you have attacked them personally, a common escape tactic people use to make themselves feel right when in fact they are wrong. You might, for example, be talking with an Analytic employee and you point out that his calculations and projections were wrong, perhaps founded on a faulty premise. That's the criticism. Follow up by mentioning how you found this lapse surprising given the quality work he did on Project X just last month. You know he is capable of excellent work like that, and you look forward to more such good work in the future. Such an ending softens the initial corrective action and reinforces in his mind that you regard him as capable and talented. He leaves with that dominant impression. You have motivated him to continue as before, you have shown him that one lapse does not make for ruin, and you have told him he is valued.

Such a tactic, ending on a positive note, is crucial everywhere. We teach officers contacting people in the streets to do everything they can **"to leave people better than you found them at their worst."** Even if an officer had had to fight to subdue a subject, his last words to that subject should be along the lines of, "Hey, maybe next time we meet we won't have to duke it out. Work with me and we'll both have less aches and pains!" I call this a "softening tactic" because in almost all cases the next time the officer meets that same individual, the violator proves to be **easier** to deal with than before. Hence the officer (and the civilian or violator) is safer. Should the officer end on a negative note: "Hey, buddy, how'd you like the beating?"—he markedly increases the chances that violence will occur again with the same subject. After all, the subject feels he has to save or regain some personal face; he will be more prepared and inclined to fight again and this time harder. Peace officers should talk the talk of peace, not violence.

So, too, should the supervisor follow the **principle of leaving his people better than he found them!** Specific praise and a word of encouragement go a long way toward bringing the best out of people. You must lift people up, and appropriate praise is perhaps the best vehicle we know to enhance another's sense of Self. Remember, of the "six selves" we carry around with us, the most important is how others see us! Everyone needs outward positive confirmation from others, and you, the supervisor, have a responsibility to help others build their most powerful self. Make a rule for yourself: never walk away from someone you are responsible for without first enhancing the other's sense of his self worth.

## CHAPTER TEN

# DISCIPLINE AND CORRECTIVE ACTION

---

As difficult as effective praise is to deliver, delivering words of correction or punishment is even more tenuous and treacherous for the supervisor or leader. The sad truth is that rarely do supervisors do a good job when they have to face one of the oldest challenges in society: What to do with people who do not play by the rules everybody else does?

In the extreme, people who violate the rules of civilized society are put in prisons but for those in any form of a leadership or management role we must find effective ways to deal with subordinates and employees who run astray of policies, procedures, and guidelines. Every parent is faced with a similar dilemma, how to discipline a child or young person properly with positive, life-building results. When people break the rules, people who live by those rules naturally get angry; it's unavoidable. Once angry, we are tempted to take our anger out on the rule breaker. We know that verbal abuse can be far more devastating than physical abuse, more lasting and permanent. We can avoid hurting our employees only by controlling our anger. We can be "hard," but as leaders we must never be hurtful.

The goal of **Verbal Judo** is control, and nowhere is control more necessary that in administering appropriate corrective action. To do it well, you must follow one unarguable principle: **Be disinterested when you correct!** Remember the state of Mushin or "no mind" so important for the police officer to handle verbal abuse? Well, you must achieve this same state before you utter one word of corrective action to another. To be "disinterested" means to be unbiased, coming from the Latin "dis" meaning "no" and the root meaning of the word "interest" meaning "biased." Many people wrongly believe being disinterested means to be uninterested; it does not. It means to be unbiased, open, and flexible, precisely the mental state needed to deliver words of correction to another.

But developing and maintaining a still center or focus when you administer corrective action can be difficult, almost unnatural. It is natural to lash out with anger and recrimination when people do not do what we expect or want them to; we let words rise readily to our lips, when angry, and when we do so we destroy any chance of achieving the GOAL of corrective action. The GOAL of any corrective action is to **make the other better**. Rehabilitation and remediation are twin objectives for the supervisor. Ironically (from a natural perspective), the goal of correcting another is positive, not negative, which means, among other things, the language in which we couch our remarks must be positive! And this is so hard when we feel like putting someone down or exacting some form of revenge. The proper *end* of discipline or correction must be positive reconstruction. Proper communication tactics and techniques can and will keep us safe within our authority role but we must remember to use them and we must remember to adhere to the principle of positive rebuilding rather than the easier, more natural, destruction of character.

Proper communication tactics and techniques work because they help us separate emotion from the act of correction. If you are wondering what is wrong with unleashing your emotions, consider this: the more you show negative emotion, the more excuses a subordinate has for not listening or changing his or her errant behavior. Once the impact of our negative emotions are felt, the subordinate can and will say, "Well, he doesn't like me anyway... this is just personal!" The employee, or child, or peer, will focus on your hurtful words *only* and not on what you are trying to achieve as a supervisor making correction actions. Anger allows people to react to your feelings rather than your corrective words, and you lose the opportunity to modify behavior once an angry word leaves your lips.

Ironically, then, showing your feelings weakens your delivery and provides an "escape route" for the person being counseled. Moreover, anger and negativism turn what must be a professional act into a personal one, thereby deleting credibility and power. To be a professional, you must use your words to properly change and modify behavior, keeping that proper distance initially given you by your rank or position. The moment you use your words in a personal manner you descend to that lower level where almost everyone feels they have a right to meet you word for word. Consider the image of parents screaming at their children, and their children screaming back. What's the difference? None. No one involved is leading. Adults must mirror a better way, the more mature way, to their children. Children learn by watching their parents. Officers learn by watching their supervisors, and employees learn by watching their managers, and all learn by watching and emulating their leaders. Much of what you teach, or fail to teach others as a leader and supervisor, is carefully observed by those you lead or manage. Mirroring the positive or negative is natural for those in subordinate roles, so be careful what you dramatize! Indeed, people want their leaders and their supervisors to be better than they are, to represent that to which they can aspire.

Communication tactics make all the difference. Without tactics your *tone* of voice (remember that demon?) will give you away, as will negative body language such as frowns, sneers, or condescending looks. Even should you be powerful enough to "watch your lips," what you actually say and present will betray your true feelings and most likely ruin any chance of making a positive impact on another. Let us say that someone in your organization has broken a rule or policy and he is referred to your office for discipline. You have read the reports from your supervisory subordinates, and the meeting with the offender takes place in your office. How do you handle it effectively, especially since you were not on the scene at the time of the alleged violation?

First, **focus only on the GOAL of discipline**: to rebuild positively! Any other focus will lead you astray. Everything you say and do **must** be in line with this goal. Say and do nothing that will detract from achieving this goal! Should you find yourself too angry at the time to control your words, too angry to focus on the goal, tactically delay any commentary concerning corrective action until you regain the proper focus. Though hard to practice, force yourself to delay and save yourself endless mistakes in dealing with people.

Now, focus on the **Specific Behavior** in question, and *never* generalize! Remember, when praising, the more specific the better; so, too, with corrective action. **Be Specific!** Generalities are rarely true, so any utterance of them will markedly detract from the truthfulness of your statements and cost you credibility with the listener. Use the specifics set forth in the reports you have before you...after you have assured yourself these are accurate and unbiased!

Next, describe the problem to your employee. In other words, **Set the Context** from leadership's point of view. Remember the Five Steps to Persuasion? Step Two was Set the Context. Do that here. Outline, using reason and accurate data, what you know, have heard or read, and then ask the other to agree or to define his or her own context. How does he or she see it, now that you have brought it up? Keep your voice calm and direct, devoid of any charged emotionalism. Such an approach clarifies the issue, an important step, and is fair in that you also listen to the other's view. The professional **ground** has now been established for your discussion. Remember, people believe they have an inalienable right to know, to be filled in on the context of the issue, and any failure to do this stimulates negative reactions and resistance. People do not have to agree with your context, but they do have a right to know. Parents are great offenders here. Too often they have the old idea that children should obey, not ask why: "I don't have to answer to my kids!" Telling people "why" is a great power, not a weakness. When you set the context, you clarify, you calm, and you come across as professional rather than personal. Too many supervisors feel their position gives them the **right** not to have to explain their actions, but they are wrong. Nothing causes low morale and dislike more than failing to fill people in on why you are taking the actions you are. So be strong; tell them!

From here you discuss the **areas of Agreement or Disagreement** between your view of the context and his, and then **define the problem** as you now see it. Your definition of the problem may well have been modified or sharpened by what you learned from the other, so define what you now see as the significant problem that must be handled or faced. Keep your voice calm, reasonable, and direct. You are defining and outlining the professional ground you both have developed.

Finally, **Present Options for Resolution,** first by discussing the options as **you** see them, and then by allowing the other to discuss these options from **his** point of view. Working this way you will more often than not be surprised by how much accord there is at this point between you and the other. Come to some form of **Resolution** and state it clearly and unequivocally; you are after all, the supervisor and must make the final decision. Here your voice must be decisive and authoritative. Because the person being admonished has had some say in the process, some ownership in the event, the chance to "be heard," there is little or no probability the other will go away unfairly angry or dissatisfied. This only occurs UNLESS you fail to **close the session on a POSITIVE NOTE!** Strive to leave your subordinate feeling better about you and himself than he might have when he walked in the door! If he can leave feeling better about you, he works harder and with more loyalty than if he left feeling put down and denigrated. Also, if he can leave feeling better about himself as an employee, he will work harder to become a better employee. Recall the advice we gave you in using Praise. If you intend to criticize, do it first, but follow up your critique with praise!

Let's imagine that you are home, on a Friday night, and you have asked your sixteen-year-old son to take the trash out before he heads off to the party. He is rushing about, obviously anxious to be on his way. His response to your request is an abrupt, "Hey, Dad, do it yourself! I'm busy! Haven't got the time!" Many parents, hearing this nasty tone and "rank insubordination" will snap, and immediately lash back with, "don't you take that tone with me or you will go nowhere!" And the fight is on!

But remember the **Five Steps** to better persuasion? Use them here, and try to be strong enough at the time to let your son's "attitude drift like a boat downstream!" Focus only on his behavior. Parents, like supervisors, often fall into the trap of being sucked in by someone's bad attitude. Teenagers can be walking embodiments of bad attitudes, as are difficult employees! One great tactic is to **separate attitude from behavior, and focus only on the behavior!** So instead of naturally reacting to son's bad attitude, you wisely move to Step Two and **Set the Context:** " Look, son, you and I had an agreement, a contract, that you would see to the trash every Friday night prior to your going anywhere, and you agreed, as did I, so why don't you just keep your word and move the cans curbside?" Now you have clarified the contract, kept your voice reasonable and calm, and he has the opportunity to obey, without losing any personal face because you have not attacked him, only reminded him.

But son resists, saying, "Hey, Dad, you know that contract isn't really fair. I don't have the time now and you do. Do it yourself!" Move now to Step Three, create and present **Options.** Again letting his attitude drift, you say, "Look, you've got some good options here. Sam next door will do it for five bucks, you know that, and your sister is inside, I'll bet she'll do it for three! Tell you what, give me two and I'll do it for you! But cans go to the curb! No cans, no party! And, I'd like to see you go to that party! You decide. Why don't you just move 'em to the curb?"

Notice here that you have offered the good options first, always the rule, and the negative second. Moreover, you have managed to make your voice sound concerned that if he does the right thing he can go out that night. No threats, no recriminations, no anger. Again, son can obey and not lose that all-important personal face. Most teenagers in our experience will take one of the offered options, though you can expect some grumbling as he hauls the cans to the curb. After all, what son will want to pay someone else money he probably needs that night?

But this time your son again resists: "Heck no, I'm not doing it and I'm not paying anyone else! I'm off to the party!" Step Four, **Confirmation** time. "Son, is there anything I can say at this time to get you to see that those cans go to the curb, I'd like to think so?" Again, notice that your voice is calm and indeed hopeful that compliance is possible, so again he can save face, grumble something like, "Yeah, say please!" and you do and he does! But, imagine a most truculent son, "Nope, Dad, no can do!" Following the 5-Step, you now must **ACT!** You must take corrective action now or lose all credibility. What you do is up to you and your culture, but a firm decision must be made and adhered to for you to fulfill the role of father (Leader and Supervisor). As you inform him of his punishment: he is going to his room, no party, for example, be sure you make your voice neutral and again devoid of anger. Why should you be angry, after all, he made his decision and the consequences follow.

The **5-Step Tactic** keeps you disinterested and focused. At each step your son has the opportunity to obey without "giving in" or losing personal face, and at all points it has been fair. Even in his room he will have to admit to himself that he had chances to go to the party and his fate lies with him alone. You, because you have adhered to the tactic, have not said or done anything for which later you might be sorry. The only way in which you could lose using this approach would be to go through the 4 Steps and then fail to ACT, Step 5. Then son would know he controls you, and your power is lost. Whenever you have to deal with a truculent employee, use the 5 Steps, and use them in the order in which we have described. Often, supervisors will go from **ask** to **options**, in their hurry, forgetting to **Set the Context**. When they do this, they lose the power of defining and clarifying the ground of the issue, and they lose that all important professional setting so necessary, should they have to later move to punishment or discipline.

The Verbal Judo approach to Leadership, its **Tao or Way**, is strategy/tactic-centered because relying on one's natural responses or good nature is unpredictable and even dangerous. Sound **Communications Strategy and Tactics** enhance your ability to deal with difficult people by keeping you professional and helping you help others save personal face even while under the guns of discipline and punishment. One of the most important truths I have learned over my thirty years in training and supervising others is this: **what you say to people and how you treat people become a part of who they are!** Isn't this scary? Think of the responsibility you have once you assume a supervisory position! Think of the damage you can do, even inadvertently, if you are not properly trained or fail to display compassionate empathy? Every time you speak from an authority position, you have immense influence and power to do good or evil.

Worse, an otherwise good leader and supervisor can destroy years of friendship and trust with a subordinate by one unthinking, uncaring, unnecessary act of improper corrective action. People who know and trust us as both friends and authority figures will not "get over it" when we improperly, unfairly, or unwisely take them to task. Those closest to us have placed great faith in us, and when faith is betrayed through anger, stupidity, pride or arrogance we, as the proponent of the same, can expect to pay a dear price.

Treat people with Respect and Dignity, and they will mirror the same back to you three times in intensity. We know from acting school that whatever the actor puts forth on stage is reflected back by the audience threefold! Such reflection accounts for why people cry at particularly good movies. Look at the general morale in any department. If it is low, it is the fault of the leaders. People reflect their leaders' attitudes and positions. Show me a department that is sloppy and inefficient, and I will show you sloppy and inefficient leadership! Show me a department head that constantly threatens his or her officers with their job security and I'll show you a department of officers and administrative staff that will wave wildly and happily when the tyrant retires, leaves for another position, or is terminated. Too often we hear supervisors complain their people don't want to work, don't have the old values, and can't be motivated. Hogwash! The people are not the problem, the leadership is!

When supervisors at all levels get this message, the morale and work productivity of their people will rise, and keep rising. Motivation (raising others' expectations) and discipline (rebuilding conduct and performance positively) go hand in hand. Criticism well done is the reverse of praise. Audiences are *made*. How you as a leader and supervisor behave in front of others dictates your audience's response. If you think you handled something well, but the employee leaves feeling you didn't, you didn't! That's the truth. An actor may feel he played his role brilliantly, but if the audience thought he was a flop, he was a flop. There is no escape from this truth!

If you truly wish to lead others, you must be wiser than they. Part of your wisdom will lie in knowing what **not** to do when you discipline or punish others. **Never admonish or insult someone in public,** in front of others. Some supervisors have told me that dressing someone down in front of his or her colleagues is good strategy because it "teaches them a lesson they will never forget." Wrong, wrong, wrong! If this form of egotistical behavior teaches any lesson, it teaches a negative one and one that never *will* be forgotten. When you put someone down in front of others, you embarrass and humiliate that person to the point where no positive learning can take place. Resentment is the only product of such behavior, and it is resentment against you! In my other books I have called this an example of "Verbal Karate," using words to hurt and puncture egos. No matter your intentions, if you punish someone publicly, you lose all credibility, with the one to whom you are speaking and with all those standing around. Others in the area are embarrassed for the subject, feel sorry for the subject, and dislike you for it. They also fear for themselves because they know that there, but for the grace of God, go they!

What kind of supervisors punish in public? Brutal, nasty ones for sure, so insecure they have to put others down in front of an audience to make themselves feel better! Power hungry ones who want to demonstrate over and over that they "run the show," again a sign of insecurity and weakness. And weak ones who, because they cringe at the thought of having to face someone, one on one, prefer to "shotgun" the group with generalities. This "shotgun discipline" syndrome is all too common. I knew a sergeant once who discovered that two of his officers had been using their patrol cars for personal business, usually following their eight-hour shifts. So he instituted a policy where all officers had to sign their cars out and sign them back in, returning their keys in person to the desk supervisor. The sergeant wasn't going to trust any of his people to take the keys at beginning of shift and return them to a box at the end, as had been the previous policy. So he went before his eleven-man squad at beginning of shift, and said, "I have evidence that **you people** have been misusing your police vehicles, running personal errands and the like, so from now on you will sign out your car keys at beginning of shift and return them to the duty sergeant at the desk at end of shift. If **you people** are going to act like children, you will be treated like children!"

What is wrong with this shotgun approach to corrective action? Much! First, the two offenders literally got away with it. They never had to account for their violations of policy. Everyone else did! The other nine officers had no idea what the sergeant was referring to and thus felt angry that they were taking the fall for something they had not done! Morale plummeted. The innocent ones felt there was no justice in the department and the entire shift grumbled and bitched the rest of the year about the unfair leadership within their team. And rightly so!

The sergeant was too weak and fearful to confront the two violators. Both officers were older and greatly respected by the department as a whole, so the sergeant found it easier to blame everyone else rather than have to face the two personally. What he should have done, of course, was to pull the two off to one side, describe what he had learned, listen to whatever they might have had to say, and then come to some appropriate discipline. He just didn't have the courage for it. My co-author and I have seen such failed leadership in academia, police work, the military and the business world, and it all stems from leadership weakness.

The powerful leader is fearless. He does his research, brings the alleged offenders before him, in private, and outlines what he knows and what he doesn't, and asks for them to provide their own perspectives on what he has found. He then goes through the steps we outlined, ending with a positive resolution. In this manner he operates from principle, not feeling, and he moves tactically to ensure a positive rebuilding of the flawed employees.

Weak and vicious supervisors not only punish in public, they put people down rather than using criticism to raise them up.

Many, indeed, get real pleasure out of humiliating someone. **Never put someone down** should be inscribed on every supervisor's desk! Concurrent with this error is the error we have pointed to earlier, where the supervisor **shows his feelings of anger** and irritation while administering corrective action. The real pro never allows his feelings to surface. He uses his words properly to address the issue at hand.

Some of you reading this may want to interject, *"But can't I ever express my feelings? Isn't it good to do this sometimes? Don't I have to be honest?"* An interesting and valid comment. The answer is, yes, you may talk with others about your feelings, but if you do, you cannot correct them. Let's imagine you are really irritated at one of your people and you want to say something to him. Do it. But do it "off the record," meaning, go and in private say something like this:

> *"Look, John, for the next few minutes I am not your supervisor, just a friend, and I want to tell you a couple of things that have been bothering me about you. You may say whatever you like in response, and it stays here, between just the two of us. OK?"*

If he says, *"yes,"* then go ahead and express whatever negative feelings you have, and allow him to do the same back to you. It's off the record, never to be reported or used against either of you. In this way you can clear the air between you and the other and not make an enemy. Indeed, these "off-the-record" chats can go a long way toward developing a trusting and open relationship with someone, or with a group. But, make a note! You must drop your role of supervisor, or father, or mother, or manager, and create an equal and level playing ground for such discussion to develop healthy results.

You cannot keep your role of leadership and also express your negative feelings. Your role is too powerful, and people will feel the hurt, and desire revenge if you attempt it. Level the playing field and be strong enough to take as well as give. What you learn might save your career!

And very important, you must **never generalize when you discipline**. Never use words like "always," "never," and "you people." Words like these always stimulate an argument because people rarely "always" or "never" do things. In reality, they occasionally stumble or misfire, and you need to address the particular violation rather than express your exasperation. Generalities detract from your truthfulness and they show you to be extreme. Precision and specificity earn your respect; they show you have **noticed** something that needs correction. Also, when you are precise in your commentary, people are forced to respond to those specifics, so the burden is on them to explain their actions. Generalities allow others to argue and equivocate.

And finally, **never threaten!** Consequences can be very usable ammunition to get someone's attention, but these should be part of the process you have used in talking about options. Tactically they are important when outlined as we have suggested above, but when consequences are phrased as threats, bad things happen. First, threats create resistance, anger, and fear— three devils you don't want to bring forth. When you threaten, you tend to phrase your commentary with an "Either-Or" statement: "Either you do this, or I'll do that!" Such statements leave people with no out, no freedom of response, so they feel trapped. Note also that such statements trap you as well. Should the subject challenge you, you must act on precisely what you said, or lose credibility. And what if, in anger or irritation, you threatened something you really can't, or shouldn't, do? Again, you lose credibility...and perhaps a truly good officer or friend.

At the very best, people threatened become defensive, and defensive people become dangerous. First, they now see you as the enemy, not as their wise leader. Second, should they know you couldn't or shouldn't make good on your threat, they will continue to test you to force your hand. I once heard a lieutenant tell a patrol officer, "You speak that way to me again and I will have you fired!" The supervisor could not fire anyone, and the officer knew it, so he continued with his insubordination and the supervisor lost face with the entire group. Another officer was threatened with an abrupt shift change if he didn't change his current course of action, and the officer went to his union rep, complained that he was being harassed, and the supervisor had to undergo an arduous series of hearings defending himself and his verbal conduct towards his troops. Threaten without the authority to carry through and you, yourself, become threatened.

Leaders and supervisors who use threats to motivate people only de-motivate them and create resistance. It's the tool of the weak. Strong leaders know the system, know what they can do and what they can't, and use options rather than threats. Consequences can and sometimes should be hard, but they must be part of a tactical dialogue, never arbitrary. Actions by the supervisor should be based on the employee's behavior, not his attitude. Attitudes can only be changed over long periods of time. The way in which you as supervisor interact with your people, over time, is the only sure way to change their attitudes for the better. Act in such a way as to make your people better.

My co-author has served as a fire-team leader, squad leader, section chief, platoon sergeant, and company size Special Forces advisor while in the military. He has overseen 1400 hourly employees for a Fortune 500 company in the area of discharge and discipline, and successfully led / managed high risk security professionals in the most violent city and country on the face of the planet (Baghdad, Iraq). In his experience as a leader and supervisor he's never seen threats create positive results. In fact, he's seen otherwise. Good and poor subordinates and employees respond favorably to leaders, managers, and supervisors who they inherently, intuitively "read" as stand-up, straight-talking, front-line men and women of Authority.

Period.

Punishment, discipline, and correction are necessary in any organization, but people with the power of management and supervision behind them must strive never to **draw blood** when they engage in such actions. The sword of correction must cut cleanly; people must be better for the experience, not worse, and the real skill lies in **caring enough** to be tough yet fair.

## CHAPTER ELEVEN

# THE ART AND GIFT OF PERSUASION

---

Actionable leadership is by its very nature the ability to persuade those working with or for you, at any level in your organization, company, department or government body to accept your vision and intent as leader, manager, or supervisor. The ability, or art, of Persuasion is winning a discussion, argument, debate, or battle without using one's force of authority. In Verbal Judo we call it gaining the voluntary compliance of the Other, or motivating by the use of words, tone, intonation, and expression someone you are in contact with to pursue one course of action (yours) over another.

In his *Ars Rhetorica*, Aristotle defined what he discovered to be four basic appeals that motivate people to take action. These are the **Ethical Appeal**; the **Rational Appeal**; the **Personal Appeal,** and the **Practical Appeal**. By defining these four in the context of Actionable Leadership via the Verbal Judo model you, as a leader, will gain an immense reservoir of leadership tools with which to properly and constructively motivate your employees, co-leaders, and even superiors to achieve those goals and objectives you are responsible for bringing to fruition.

## Ethical Appeal

This form of Persuasion is grounded in your reputation and credibility as both a private person and a workplace professional. The Ethical Appeal's foundation, or Ground Zero, is rooted in who your people see and know you to be by your actions and behavior both on and off the court. If your reputation is known to be ethical, moral, honest, trustworthy, and fair-minded, this form of persuasive appeal encourages people to do what you ask of them because they trust you. Further, they want to be like, and be liked by, you because you are who and what you model in your personal and professional life. They aspire to reflect back to you what you show them as a leader. There is no more difficult yet simpler form of leadership and persuasion than this.

In the workplace your professional presence, seen and felt by others you come in contact with by whatever means, is your most powerful tool and weapon. We all can recall leaders we have worked with, or for, in the past that we would have followed anywhere, at anytime, to accomplish what often seemed impossible. We possessed this deep feeling of loyalty and belief in such people because we were taught by their example to us to believe in them regardless of the challenge or the odds. This is the Ethical Appeal in action and practice. Such leaders are not infallible and certainly they stumble and fail during the course of their careers. However, such leaders, those who command by Ethical Appeal, have also mastered the art of overcoming their personal and professional shortcomings, or failures, and turned them into rich lessons for all to learn from. In other words the Ethical Appeal requires extraordinary personal responsibility on the part of its practitioner.

The Achilles tendon, if you will, of the Ethical Appeal is its adherence to consistency. Leadership pursuing this form of persuasion must be consistent in act and deed, and can never present a false front or image in order to accomplish the goal of voluntary compliance. The Ethical Appeal enlists the category of individual and leader who is believed by his subordinates, co-leaders, and superiors to truly and earnestly want the very best possible for the Whole, and who actively and daily seeks to ensure both group and individual growth, expansion, and success by pursuing right courses of action in and outside of the workplace.

Police officers are a work force by profession whose credibility (Public Trust) is based on their ethical appeal as both individuals and as a department or agency. A police officer is expected to model and adhere to legal, ethical, and moral standards that our society promotes as necessary for good social order and behavior. He or she then must rely on the Ethical Appeal daily, as it is the core of the profession. When a police officer desires people to act in the manner he requests or directs by lawful order, his most powerful tool at that moment is his ethical presence. He, by the authority and power delegated him by law with those additional caveats of a commitment to high ethical and moral standards, becomes his own best advocate for the correct action to be taken by those he is governing at the moment. A proper police professional will be educated by his department to understand that he can appeal to John Q. Public, not only by his own ethical presence but also through the ethical presence of his department.

Needless to say the two must be in concert with each other for the best possible presentation.

Most of us will do the right thing once it is presented properly to us. Any of the personality styles described in this book possesses a powerful desire to act according in concert with accepted and laudable values. Indeed, value-based action, or behavior, is attractive to people. Still, there is a segment of society that requires us as leaders to persuade them by demonstrating a value-based reason for their voluntary compliance. We have all experienced those individuals who chaff at certain tasks and responsibilities, whether to society or in the workplace, because they cannot find or see the value reason for supporting, through voluntary compliance, these requirements. The Ethical Appeal relies on your ethical presence to take the time and make the effort to set the standard, educate the management and work group you are leading, and then follow through with your people as they perform what it is you desire to be accomplished. Again, the Ethical Appeal is successful because it inspires through a respected and trusted leader the best individual and group performance possible by those affected. This appeal requires the infusion of real meaning and true value by a leader whose ability lies in the successful execution of the Ethical Appeal.

During the writing of this book we learned of a law enforcement professional who believed that police officers could lie as long as they did not lie while under oath. This philosophy was shared with both his supervisors and the patrol ranks at various times and in various circumstances. In time, many of the officers and administrative staff of the department the man was responsible for, came to mistrust both he and their fellow officers and employees. Why? Because their initial trust in the department's leadership was eroded by perceived examples that what he said was not necessarily credible. Soon the mid-level management of the department began not only mistrusting the senior administrator but also the patrol ranks. If the department philosophy by virtue of the department head's position on truth-telling was that cops could lie as long as they weren't sworn before a court, then their subordinates were probably fibbing about anything that during the course of their duty day might get them in trouble if they 'fessed up. This attitude then began being vocalized between the mid-level managers and supervisors and the patrol and administrative staffs. As no one enjoys being called a liar, the finger pointing and counter accusations flew. Now the supervisors were "liars" and seeking only to make trouble for the rank and file. Inter-department memos flew and complaints were filed both internally and through union channels. In the end no one trusted anyone and gradually this mistrust made its way into the local law enforcement circles as well as the courts, the prosecutor's office and defense lawyers' offices, and finally onto the street where John Q. Public lived and worked.

All because one senior administrator compromised the basis of the Ethical Appeal by promoting the mistaken position that cops, his cops, could lie as long as they didn't do so under oath.

Now, perhaps, the man meant to say that in the profession of police work there are legally sanctioned activities where a cop can "lie" in the pursuit of his or her investigation. Certainly the difficult and dangerous job of working narcotics requires police officers to fabricate stories, characters, roles, and excuses in order to get at the truth and to protect their very lives. This form of professional deception or "lying" is understood by our legal system and can stand up in court, when such story telling is conducted within the parameters of law and those legal decisions clarifying the need and application of such deceptions. But to our understanding this narrow interpretation of professional deceit within the scope of law enforcement is not what was placed in proper context when the subject department head's statements were uttered.

Cops, according to him, are like anyone else when it comes to lying until they are sworn under oath to tell the truth.

Wrong message sent, wrong message received.

At the other end of the ethical spectrum there is the sheriff of a large county who, upon taking office, made it quietly clear that any deputy working for him who was caught lying, stealing, or cheating could expect termination. This senior administrator possessed a long and carefully crafted professional history of sound ethical and moral behavior. He'd come up through the ranks and had gone the extra mile to educate himself and then others on proper police ethics, behavior, and performance. By his example he began cultivating a new department culture beginning with the re-education of his senior and mid-level management teams. Soon the word began trickling down as to what was expected, what would be rewarded, and what would

happen if sound law enforcement ethics and behavior were mis-
managed, overlooked, ignored, or violated. After several inner-
departmental discharge and disciplinary actions, and at least one
very public (and successful) criminal prosecution, the power of the
Ethical Appeal began to have an impact not only throughout the
department but out in the community as well. Cops were not
above the law, not exempted from accepted law enforcement
ethics, and expected to uphold high personal and professional
morals in order to practice their chosen profession.

In short, lying was not okay whether under oath or not, and
neither were any of a hundred other pitfalls an officer of the law
can fall prey to, unless a clear path is made for him by his
leadership as he walks his career beat in the Public's trust.

Actionable leadership demands higher vision of the leader
who desires success at the forefront. Without higher vision and its
ethical and moral support systems we all fall prey to the lowest
common denominator or degrees of action and behavior. For
police officers this means mirroring the law-breakers of society by
word and deed, and for those others in the public and private
sectors of society it means lower productivity, high employee
turnover, marginal quality of services and goods, a demoralized
work force, and finally failure at the leadership level to raise its
people and products up to become the most they possibly can be.

## Rational Appeal

This appeal relies on the use of Reason and Logic. A segment
of any work force or management team believes their opinions,
views, and actions are logically sound and based on reason. Of our
previously discussed personality types the Analytical Personality
is surely one of these. However few of us wish to be seen as acting
on unsound principle, or illogical reasoning. Ask any of us at any
time of the day and we will tell you whatever it is we are doing at
the moment is being done "for a good reason." A common
leadership – supervisory trap is to sincerely believe that if we, as
a management figure, can only show people that what we want
them to do just makes good sense, they will accept our rationale
and simply "Do it." All too often we are proven dramatically
wrong.

Make a note! Of the four Appeals the Rational Appeal is the
**weakest sister in the bunch**. You're surprised? Consider this.

When people in general are angry, upset, frustrated they do not and cannot appreciate reason or logic. Indeed they have no patience with either! How many times has a spouse offered during a discussion or argument, "Why can't you be more reasonable?" How many times has the response, most often angry, been, "Reasonable? I AM being reasonable, dammit!" Telling, or demanding, or suggesting that someone become reasonable under such circumstances is as ineffective as telling someone to calm down. Again, police officers on the street dealing with all too often angry, frustrated, often dangerous people make this mistake and the result is always less than calm. One of Thompson's Laws is this: "Never tell someone to calm down or to be more reasonable; make them calmer and therefore reasonable by the way in which you handle them."

The Rational Appeal requires data, evidence, facts, and proof. People at odds are not receptive to these factors in the Rational equation. When people, or an employee or subordinate, are upset and on the defensive they literally cease hearing you. Common sense and reason are out the window and the more you extort the virtues of both, the angrier and more uncommunicative your audience will become. For example, when is the last time your spouse sat down with you and tried to discuss why you cannot simply write checks like they are going out of style? With checkbook and cancelled checks in hand (data, evidence, and proof of your imprudence) the conversation is meant to remind you, perhaps, of past agreements to be thriftier and less spontaneous with the family funds. However the most common response to such a confrontation is defensive, with anger a close second. Listening to your spouse's probably sound and reasonable verbal essay is stopped dead in its tracks. You know your financial partner is right, but being right doesn't necessarily make it so! "There was a darned good reason for me buying that $500 snowboard!" you retort, "and what about that worthless new dining room table you bought without asking me!"

Good reasons are not necessarily logical reasons. Often they are actually emotional reasons and emotional responses, like oil and water, do not mix with rational responses. The Rational Appeal will only have power when all parties involved are calm and prepared to listen *rationally* to a discussion or order or directive or presentation. Only when this environment exists or is created by you, the leader, are your employees, co-managers or supervisors, or subordinates capable of appreciating common sense and logical reasoning.

A rational appeal for voluntary compliance, the goal of actionable leadership, is to clarify the issue or matter at hand. We will most always fail when we rely upon facts, figures, data and evidence as ammunition meant to shoot down our audience. In the Rational Appeal you, as a leader, must always first create a calm and interactive environment. You are not there to win an argument or debate, you are there to set the parameters and provide the guidance for "the way ahead." Upon creating a positive environment for your audience you can then introduce logic, reason, your data, and why all of this leads to the conclusion you've reached as to how to proceed, or why your audience should support your call for their full cooperation and support.

When using the Rational Appeal you must be cautious. When people make a mistake based on an error in their reason or data, you must understand they will most likely be (and become) defensive as you seek to correct, as opposed to challenge, them. Establishing good rapport with someone who has made it their life's goal to be "right" on every subject they involve themselves in, is critical to success when dealing with them. Such folks pride themselves on being accurate and sound in their approach, so either word or implication that sends a message that their work was careless or inaccurate must be avoided. The wise leader will actually lead the adherent to rational thought and problem solving to discover his or her own mistakes! After all, there is joy in self-discovery, too. If you as the leader or manager of someone who is a rational thinker, planner, and doer can bring them to their own conclusion that their error was in their reasoning or data process, you will solve your own problem with them and at the same time avoid making an enemy or becoming engaged in meaningless wrangling and argument.

The third appeal is the **Personal Appeal** and it is the **second most powerful** appeal we can use when working with, or leading people.

## Personal Appeal

This appeal is based on the **selfish interests** of the other. People have a wonderful way of doing what it is we would like them to when we, as leaders, can show them that doing so is in their best interests. Meaning, they will somehow personally benefit from following our plan. The Personal Appeal is an option-based approach to problem solving and actionable leadership. You, as a Verbal Judo leader, will carefully study the situation you are seeking to resolve or direct, and create a workable collection of viable options from which you want your audience to choose from. You always offer the best options to them first! This is exactly the opposite approach the majority of leaders and managers pursue today when dealing with their people. The "Here's what's going to happen to you if you don't do this..." formula is non-productive and only works in the short term if it works at all. None of us enjoys or seeks being threatened, especially by someone for whom we are working. The Personal Appeal requires you as a leader to take the time to discover, through **Tactical Empathy,** the selfish best interests of one of your subordinates, employees, or work groups and then capitalize on this discovery by presenting right up front how they can best achieve their goal by following your lead.

Few of us will consciously go against our best interests or desires. This is even more so once someone points out, with accuracy, what these interests or desires might be. Create the right scope of Options when using the Personal Appeal, present it properly (in the right context), and let the person you are appealing to choose what he or she feels or believes is in their best (selfish) interests. In the end it is your need as a leader that is likewise fulfilled, as well.

Persuasion is not reason.

Persuasion is the unique combination of the two most powerful appeals we know of—the **Ethical Appeal** and the **Personal Appeal.** To successfully persuade someone you must be credible, and this may mean establishing your credibility at the onset by demonstrating you are believable. Remember most people we work with do not truly know us personally. At best they know we exist somewhere "up the ladder" or in their chain of command. You will often be called upon to meet with your employees or subordinates for essentially the first time they've ever dealt with you face to face. Or perhaps you have "town hall meetings" where the group has one opportunity a week, or a month, or a quarter to interact with you. Persuasion lies in your ability as an actionable leader to immediately generate a sense in your audience that you are believable and, therefore, *potentially* credible.

If you cannot transmit these two messages within minutes of meeting your audience you will not sell anyone anything. If your subordinate or employee does not believe you have their best (selfish) interests at heart any one of the Four Appeals you may try to invoke will fall on deaf ears!

The building of personal and professional credibility (and hence believe-ability) is a process of both time and consistent work. It is a process of falling down, picking yourself back up, moving forward, falling down again, and pressing on. No leader or manager is perfect, just as no subordinate is perfect. It's how we handle our imperfections that make the difference in how people see us, and where we ultimately end up in our personal and professional lives. **Actionable leadership—Verbal Judo leadership—seeks to create positive ways for people to act on our words.** Choosing the best Appeal requires the use of empathy so we can "see" what our people see...and feel what our people feel. When this process is applied to Persuasion the essential building blocks of credibility and believe-ability are laid. From this point on it is only a matter of navigating through the appeal process toward your ultimate goal or objective, channeling right actions and responses from your people toward the common good.

We tell our police audiences that **"if a person has something to gain or lose, you have something to use!"** All too often in law enforcement this truism is perverted to mean "if you threaten someone with their freedom they'll do or say what you want them to." Wrong! Make a note here. **Tactical empathy is** the real secret of Persuasion. Use and rely on the proper application of personal and professional empathy to find the most appropriate Appeal for the personality types we have defined in this book and you, as an actionable leader, will enjoy extraordinary results (success) in your position.

The final Appeal is the **Practical Appeal.**

### Practical Appeal

This is, in most cases, the last resort. Its weakness is that it *must work.* It is based on what is the most practical solution or direction to arrive at and then take. It requires the appropriate use of humor and offbeat strategies to sell it. This, then, requires a manager or leader who has a developed sense of style in these two areas if the Practical Appeal is to work. If you are not a humorous type, or humor has never worked for you, the Practical Appeal will be a tough sell. This holds true for use of offbeat strategies, or "thinking out of the box." Again, if these two approaches to your personal or professional lives are uncomfortable or unworkable for you, best to not try them out on your employees when trying to direct them!

The key that turns the lock when applying the Practical Appeal is the use of broken rhythm. **Broken rhythm** is an essential component in the martial arts. It means, in essence, to do something that is out of the ordinary in order to change the course of what might be predicted events. For example, a classically trained karate man or woman will learn, then follow, and then expect specific responses and reactions whether sparring for sport or in a street fight. This category of fighter seeks to establish within the parameters of the art he practices a cadence, or rhythm by which to engage in the battle. Once the battle rhythm is established the karate man seeks to end the competition or fight by using those techniques, in rhythm, to vanquish his opponent.

The use of broken rhythm seeks to disrupt the classical fighter's strategy. The man or woman who uses broken rhythm in their approach to either a martial arts competition, a street fight, or a business meeting or interview will first know how the opposition has trained and hence what their predictable battle rhythm will be. He then disrupts this battle rhythm by **not** doing what is expected at key or critical points in the engagement, whether on the dojo floor or in the boardroom. Once the classically trained or conditioned (martial arts or business) student, employee or subordinate is broken out of his established "beat," the broken rhythm strategy becomes a powerful tool or weapon to overcome him.

Bruce Lee, one our most talented and accomplished martial artists, believed broken rhythm training and application were essential in defeating one's opponents. He wrote the traditional martial arts with their dependence on routine and predictability of movement and action / reaction had turned them into a "classical mess." So it is with the proper application of the Practical Appeal—to be effective it relies on broken rhythm techniques meant to surprise (in a nice way) and soften (again, in a nice way) your audience's pre-conceived, pre-trained actions and reactions to you as their manager or leader.

Broken rhythm in the context of this book means we must do something out of the ordinary to change the course of events. This appeal is dependent on your creativity and empathy for others, your ability to anticipate what may work from the other person's point of view, and how you can sell your vision of what is a practical solution or direction to your audience regardless of where they might be on the organizational ladder.

The Practical Appeal is a catchall in response to difficult and challenging people as well as events. To use this Appeal successfully you must be flexible and prepared to vary (broken rhythm) your approach in an instant! Its use may range from an officer reading a newspaper in the middle of a domestic dispute to draw the attention positively onto himself and off the potential combatants, to convincing a frightened woman that her house can be exorcized of the demons that haunt it (she thinks!). I have done both successfully! This Practical Appeal is the extreme of the ability to **"Chameleon-up"** and become "who one has to be to handle the situation!"

Indeed, brilliant Persuasion mandates all four Appeals and the ability to switch tracks as soon as you sense you are losing your audience. The rule of thumb is to vary the Appeal as soon as you meet resistance in your interactions. The student and then master of actionable leadership are prepared to shift his or her angle of persuasion (attack) at a moment's notice. Being flexible, or open to what is going on around you or being sent as an unspoken message or signal, as well as said, is primary. Once a fighter or martial artist stops moving and becomes rooted in one place, regardless of his skill or plan, he becomes available to be hit and possibly with that one knockout punch or kick!

The same holds true in the use **of Persuasion** via the tools of the **Four Appeals.**

## CHAPTER TWELVE

# HOW TO DIAGNOSE A VERBAL ENCOUNTER

A rmed with the **Four Appeals**, you are now ready to sharpen your diagnostic and evaluative skills with regard to how to **read** a verbal encounter **while being in the midst of one.** Nowhere in the colleges and universities do we teach students how to analyze a verbal encounter. I guess professors assume that we will figure out verbal encounters as we go. Sometimes this holds true, if we are lucky, but remember, **"Luck favors the Prepared Mind!"**

We now offer you a simple problem-solving **heuristic** that will enable you to be much more effective in talking and persuading others. Persuasion, or Rhetoric as we call it, is indeed a skill one can and should master, and as a supervisor you must be continuously skillful in persuading all kinds of different and difficult people.

The acronym **P.A.C.E.** stands for the four basic ingredients of any verbal encounter.

    **"P"**    stands for the Problem
    **"A"**    for the Audience you are speaking with or before
    **"C"**    for the Constraints to effective communication present in the scene at the moment, and
    **"E"**    for your Ethical Presence as speaker.

**P.A.C.E.** becomes an internal checklist that allows you to analyze scenes and to create disinterest while in the midst of potential conflict. Once defined and illustrated, you will discover that you can use the acronym quickly and efficiently to find flexible ways to respond to your people, and maintain your calm professional manner, two traits that will markedly enhance your reputation as a leader of others.

Whenever you attempt to persuade someone, there will always be a **problem** at issue, but the real skill lies in breaking the Problem into its two basic parts, how **YOU** see it and how the *other* sees it. Almost never will these be the same, and often, they will be radically different! In my *Gentle Art of Persuasion* book, Chapter 18, I describe a hostage scene in which a man holds a knife to the throat of his young son, threatening to kill him because he is "possessed of the devil." I, as the responding officer, obviously see the man as the problem. He is sick, dangerously so. But, the man doesn't see it that way. He thinks his boy is sick, and must be cured. I call the first definition of the problem, my **Professional Problem**, and I call the man's definition the **Rhetorical Problem.** You have to solve your professional problem, yes, but the trick here is to always begin with the other's definition of the problem. If you do not, you will have conflict, argument, and no forward movement towards resolution.

If the deranged man thought his son was possessed of the devil, he was! As a rule, whenever there exists a conflict between you and the other in terms of the "reality" of the situation, **you must begin with his view**. Using Empathy, then, you can discover the full context of what he thinks, and then, using the materials of his "ground," find the appropriate options he might take to alleviate the situation. Put another way, if an employee is "out in left field" with his thinking, you must first go to his part of the field and begin the dialogue there. We call this definition of the problem the Rhetorical Problem because it is the beginning of where you will find some connection to make an impression and begin your persuasion in an effort to bring the person around to a point where you can solve your problem.

As a supervisor, your responsibility is to discover ground on which you and the subordinate, or a superior, can agree. People who are upset are not prepared to help you with this, so you must stand in the other's shoes long enough to find the connecting threads between your positions. Many supervisors think it is up to the subordinate to make this effort, but, as we pointed out in the Personality Styles chapter, Chapter Seven, it is up to you as the leader to make these efforts. Again, you must "chameleon up" to the situation and the person involved if you hope to have positive interaction and influence with the other.

Once you have defined as accurately as possible the Rhetorical Problem, you must then analyze the other as **AUDIENCE**. It is helpful and indeed correct to regard people as audiences to your performance whenever you attempt to persuade them, and we know several important things about people as audiences. One, and perhaps most critical, remember that people are **different** than you, even if you are extremely close to them. You can never assume the other will agree with you. Rather than let this difference annoy you, consider it natural and a positive challenge. Indeed, beware of people who always seem to think the way you do; they are probably playing you! Arm yourself from the start with the positive view that difference is healthy and good.

People are not only naturally different, they also **watch us** perform before them, as does any audience. Remember what we told you about audiences—they reflect back to you what you present, three times in intensity! This can be good or bad, depending upon your performance. The good actor always plays to his audience, as should you. Estimate what relations can exist between you and the other, the audience, and project into the other's world long enough to find the terms of your appeal. Identify, for example, what role the other is playing and attempt to stand in effective relation to that role using an appropriate counter-role. In considering how to handle the deranged man, for example, it was clear to me that our values were wholly different. He believed in the Devil and I didn't, but in order to get "a hearing" I had to initially adopt his value thinking and his context.

Because people are audiences to your performances, **they change** as you come before them! As any Commander or Chief must be aware, as he enters a room where his people are sitting around talking, the entire room changes with his entrance, dramatically! To make an accurate "reading" of your people, you must always remember that what you are seeing is not what was there just prior to your entrance. Some changes are being made, even as you stand there. Good street cops know this, too, or they should be taught this if they don't. As they enter a bar on a bar check, for example, the entire bar changes with their appearance, and failure to note this can mean an officer will miss the suddenly hidden dope or gun, or possibly get hurt because he failed to note subtle changes of physical movement within the bar as he entered it. People are not as they seem, but as they want you to see them. People either change as you enter their space, or they prepare a change as they enter yours. In both cases, you must remember the actor-audience connection, and estimate accordingly.

Having position and power over others is akin to having a camera as you approach people. The moment you hold the camera up, everyone changes. They either freeze, or they begin to over-act to cover their nervousness, or they play to the camera! Because of your reputation or perceived power, people always make some changes as you face them, so learn to use your projected power wisely.

Perhaps the most important point of audiences to remember is as Aristotle said, they are **made things**. You have the power to make one or more persons become what you want them to be; as you act in front of others, so you constitute your audience. Hence, as we pointed out earlier, whatever the morale is in your division, take credit for it. You created it. Whatever the work ethic is in your department, take credit for it. Stop blaming others for low morale or low productivity. Failure or success lies entirely with the leadership.

Once you have a clear idea of your Professional Problem and the Rhetorical Problem, and you have a good feel of your Audience, you must then focus your attention on the **CONSTRAINTS** that exist between you and that audience that might make communication difficult. Constraints are obstacles to effective communication, and they can be anything, from the past, the present, or the future. Too often as we talk to people we tend to forget that we have a history with them; we tend to think each encounter is unique and new, or should be. In our organizations, as in families, we lug the baggage of previous encounters in with us. We may have helped create these obstacles, or we may simply be faced with them because of what others may have done to the subject in the past. Moreover, the present encounter may have within it numerous problems created by the present moment itself. An officer, for example, trying to talk with a subject and seeking to generate voluntary compliance may find his work complicated by numerous bystanders who are egging the subject on to resist. The officer then has to deal with that constraint, either by taking the subject away from the competing audience, or by removing those people prior to resuming his persuasion. The competing audience creates "noise" that must be handled. To keep our metaphor, the stage has to be cleared before the officer can continue with his role of mediator. Whatever the case, whenever you meet resistance with someone, ask yourself, "Why is this person being so difficult? What is present that may be hindering effective communication?" Just posing these questions will give you added insight into how to handle a situation.

Over the years, I have come to believe there are three ways to handle constraints: Ignore them, Step Around them, or Use them! I discovered as a Peace Officer that people don't always like cops, so I learned early on to ignore the common insults thrown my way. I saw them as tactics used by street people to upset my balance and gain the upper hand. As cops must learn to deflect personal insults, so people in the workplace must learn to deflect snide or nasty remarks that customers, employees, and management will make. Personal insults are the first line of defense for people who want to resist our authority, so ignore them, or deflect them, and move beyond them.

But some constraints or obstacles cannot be ignored. Like a boulder in the middle of a forest path, you cannot just ignore it, but you can Step Around it! Such was the case when the deranged man said to me, "But I can't trust you, you're a cop!" Obviously I cannot ignore that comment, but I found a quick way around it by saying, "I understand that, but in this case I can't really do anything for you, only a Priest can help you, and I know of such a person. Let him help you." Obstacles that can be stepped around are things that cannot be solved at the moment; they exist, and we recognize they exist, but we need to move by them. Past experience is a wellspring of such obstacles. I once had a supervisor who had on one occasion failed me, having given me his word he would not. When he again asked for my cooperation, I reminded him that we had a bad experience earlier with regard to his word. He told me that he regretted that but the powers above him had mandated a different course of action and over-ruled him. He had more power this time to make things happen, and hoped I would give him another chance. Though still wary, I went along with him. He had stepped around part of our past—a constraint—and had enlisted my help again. He didn't fail me this time. Part of what made me compliant was his honesty in admitting a past failure. We all fail at some point, but it is how we handle failure that sets us apart from the norm.

Part of being a good supervisor lies in knowing what you can set aside or step around, and what you can't. Some employees, because they lack the larger picture of an operation, will focus on minor areas to find their complaints and bases of resistance. As a leader, with the larger vision, it is your responsibility to provide that larger overview to your people. Clarifying context puts the entire picture into perspective for the employee, and with this new perspective the employee can begin to understand why he is being asked to do a particular task.

If you cannot ignore an obstacle or step around one quickly, your third option is to **use the obstacle itself** to solve the problem. Often the solution to a problem lies in the problem itself. I have found, again and again, that what may make an initial dialogue so difficult is in fact a clue to its solution, if only it can be seen.

With my crazy man who wanted to kill his son, for example, his presentation was so shocking, initially, that it took me several minutes of fumbling around verbally before I saw that indeed he had given me the clue as to how to handle him in the very opening. He believed in the Devil and thought he had to kill his son to cleanse him of the Devil's influence. But in that same context, exorcism is an equally viable alternative to police intervention with the added benefit of saving his son's life. He thought he had to kill his son to save him. I pointed out he could save his son by having a priest exorcise his boy, thus ridding his son's soul of the Devil's influence, and cleansing him forever. My persuasion worked, and he put the knife down and came quietly. We got him the psychological help he needed and saved the boy's life, both part of my Professional Problem, and we solved his problem (the one that existed in his head) as well. The boy was "cured." The very secret of how to handle this man lay in his extreme context. I ended up using that very context to solve the problem.

Remember we mentioned earlier that when people are upset or angry, they unwittingly will give us clues as to how to handle them. We know it is important to listen carefully to our subordinates and employees because somewhere in their outbursts they will give us our persuasive ammunition. Imagine an angry contractor at your front desk screaming at you that someone gave him bad directions to the payroll office and now he can't get his check because the office is closed for the day. He rants and raves, calling you an idiot, and telling you he only has one day a week to come by the office, and he needs to be paid for work he has done for the company. Your problem is how to get him calm enough to come into your office so you can make some calls to see how he can be helped. What will you use? First, you will recall that when angry, people never say what they mean. In all his rudeness and anger what he means is, "I need some help!" So you deflect the abuse, and focus on his meaning.

Fortunately, he has in his rant given you two crucial items to use in your persuasive argument: one, he wants to be paid; and two, he only has one day a week to come down to your building. You use these two points to quiet him. What had made him mad is also what will calm him, once you point out you can help him now, only if he stops yelling and cooperates with you. You use his selfish interest (the Personal Appeal)—he wants his money—to get his attention. The constraints to effective communication with this contractor were two: a time constraint, and a need for money. Both become part of your solution.

No matter how skillfully you present your position, nothing will work if you do not present the appropriate **ETHICAL PRESENCE** throughout the encounter. Throughout my dealings with the deranged man I had to show a continuous ethical presence of concern. I was saying in effect, "I'm working with you sir, listen to me. I can help you." Nowhere would it have been appropriate to show what might have been my more natural feelings, "Hey, you're crazy! What's the matter with you!" The presence you project must be your Professional Face, that face that will best accomplish the task at hand. Whatever face will work is the one you must adopt, but the other must always feel you to be sincere and well meaning. With the angry contractor you would want to exude a caring attitude, a concerned face, and a strong "I can help you" voice. Again, as so often in this book, notice our stress on becoming who you have to be to handle the problem. Putting on the right face to meet the faces you meet is critical to your success with others, and it defines the essence of your Ethical Presence. Your believability as speaker is everything when it comes to persuading others to act as you would have them act. Your ethical **presence** (and it is just that, **a presence!**) is your Ethical Appeal, projected and felt by others, and it is your strongest tactic with difficult people.

The acronym **P.A.C.E.**, then, becomes a tactic you can use to diagnose a scene quickly and effectively to find the best terms of appeal. As an **internal checklist**, it helps you stay calmer and more analytical longer than anyone you will face. You have four crucial questions you can ask, quickly, under pressure: 1) How does this person see the problem? 2) How is he or she different from me? 3) What is making this person so difficult to deal with at this particular moment? And 4), What kind of presence must I project to be believable and credible? Just asking these questions keeps you professionally disinterested and focused.

Moreover, asking yourself these questions helps you garner the material you need to marshal a strong persuasive argument. Instead of **reacting** to people's outbursts you are **responding** to their problems, tactically and professionally. This approach guides your thinking and your actions. The goal of Verbal Judo is to benefit both parties in a confrontation. Use **P.A.C.E.** with your spouse and with your children. Use it in the workplace whenever you meet resistance. As a problem-solving tool, a heuristic, **P.A.C.E.** is a strategic way to see what lies beneath the surface of resistance. Use it to help you **pace** your way through a difficult encounter.

## CHAPTER THIRTEEN

# THE FOUR CRITERIA FOR ACTION

---

Now that you have a grip on some crucial persuasive techniques, such as the Five-Step Hard Style, the Personality Profiles, the Four Appeals, and a tactic to analyze verbal encounters, P.A.C.E., we would like to offer you some help in making good decisions regarding how to think about the practical problems you will face in your supervisory work. One of the great weaknesses in our grooming people to take supervisory positions is our failure to teach such aspirants how to think!

My own university training of over nine years had but one course that even approached this subject. The numerous supervisor courses I have since participated in or witnessed had none. Some people are more naturally analytic and thoughtful than others, true, but when you are elevated to a position of decision-making that affects others, you had best be very good at thinking through questions of means and ends.

Whenever you have to consider what to do in the real world, you are faced with what I call Matters of Practice questions. What we offer you here are four criteria you should consider before taking action or recommending action to others. These four criteria will help you to listen to others who have proposals they wish to put before you for consideration. Instead of being swept off your feet by their slick presentations, you will have a tool to analyze the quality of their thought. I remember in college when class leaders would argue for this or that, I was often swayed by one's presentation over another's, often wondering how one could really tell whose ideas were best. You will have similar trouble listening to your commanders, chiefs, and subordinates if you do not have a problem-solving tool to discern whose argument is truly better than others. The tool we provide you will not only enable you to listen more analytically to others, it will also help you marshal your own arguments concerning what should be done within the organization. Using this tool will markedly cut down on resistance from others, as you will have covered all your analytical bases. Those of you with good, creative ideas will find this heuristic exciting to use.

Whenever you wish to recommend what should be done in the workaday world, you must consider four criteria, best remembered by the acronym P.E.E.V.

You must always ask yourself are the means being proposed Practical? If you are listening to someone who argues for a particular course of action, ask yourself whether what he is recommending is feasible and practical. That is, can we do this given the available resources at hand? If you are advancing a course of action, be sure you show that what you want can be done given the materials present. One of the things that make proposals "unrealistic" to others is their knowledge that what you are asking for cannot be done without wide scale changes in the resources at hand. I once knew a lieutenant who argued vigorously that every officer should have his own personal computer. A good idea, except at the time, in the mid-eighties, there simply was not money enough for such a venture, either for the machines or the necessary training that such a proposal would entail, and he was soundly turned down.

But, for the moment, let's assume that you do have the resources available to pursue the means you want, then you have to be sure to show that these means are Efficient, meaning they can be done economically. Keep in mind the "triple ME" formula: Maximum Efficiency, Maximum Effectiveness, with a Minimum amount of Energy. Any means that calls for a maximum use of energy will probably be denied. People don't want to work any harder than they have to, and any proposal that seems to add extra effort will be resisted. I have witnessed more than one proposal become policy that so added to the paperwork of the employees that it ultimately failed, and caused a great deal of turmoil in the process. The policy had its merits, but the people who proposed it had not considered the extra paperwork (read: work and resources) it would entail.

Any policy that is not efficient causes problems. Should you believe, however, that despite your proposal being somewhat inefficient is it nevertheless necessary, be sure you make this point! It's potential inefficiency will be worth the final product or result. Do not try to hide or minimize any defect. Admit it, describe it, and show that despite such your proposal has merit and is worth pursuing. Such an approach always blunts your opposition's comebacks!

If you show your ideas to be Practical and Efficient, you must then show that these same ideas are Efficacious, meaning you can show these means will, in fact, produce the desired result. Politicians are known for telling us what we should do, but they rarely demonstrate that what they say will happen, will! Saying so never made it so! In any means you argue for, you must be prepared to show that these means will in fact produce what you say they will, and not something else! In the early 1900's, New York City outlawed the newly invented automobile because of the pollutants caused by the gasoline engines. Only horses were to be allowed in the inner city. It was not long before New Yorkers realized this new policy simply resulted in a different kind of pollution! Cars made a comeback!

As you listen to others advance their ideas about what your department should be doing, watch to see if they ever actually show you, or prove to you, that what they argue will happen, will. Make them demonstrate the relationship between the means they are arguing for and the ends they say will result. Rarely do people cover this base. Questions like, "What evidence do you have that X will produce Y," or "Where else can you see this relationship between X and Y work?" are good questions for you to pose to the presenters. Something is efficacious if it actually works, produces what you say it will. And, even if they can show you it has efficacy, probe to see what other results might also be a by-product of their means. Often these by-products are worse than the best imagined results! Remember the horses in New York City!

Lastly, ask, are the means being proposed, consonant with prevailing Values? These values can be large societal values, departmental and organizational values, or personal values, but any proposal that runs counter to existing values will run into stiff resistance. Regarding personal values, remember your Personality Styles. Any proposal that seems illogical or "slick" will meet great resistance from the Analytical, who values things that are solid and definitive. Any proposal that seems to make life more difficult for people will anger the Amiable, for he values human relationships, and any proposal whose means seem ponderous or slow moving will irritate the Driver and the Expressive who place great value on quick, decisive action and results. Each Personality Style values something different, so the more you can show that your proposal accounts for or covers the basic values of each, the better chance of finding acceptance to your ideas.

Thompson's Law: **"Right Message, Wrong Person, Game Over!"** Remember that "delivery style" is 93% of your effectiveness, so no matter how skillful or solid your argument may be, if it is not "dressed" in the correct language for the audience, you minimize your chances of finding acceptance. Let me give you an example. I wanted once to buy 160 acres of land for an investment. It had beautiful trees and meadows, and could be subdivided into four, forty-acre parcels to be resold for a profit. I faced the problem of convincing my wife, Pam, that the investment was a good one. I am an Expressive Driver, so without thinking, I said to her, "The land is just beautiful! Great for horses, beautiful views of the Sangre De Cristo Mountains, and has so many trees we could always go out there and cut our Christmas trees and dig up trees for our yard." Pam, being a Driver Analytic, said, "We can buy our Christmas trees at the market and trees are readily available, without all that effort and expense, at the local nursery!"

I had made my appeal as an Expressive! Although I had mentioned the purchase as an investment, I more naturally stressed the aesthetic appeal. My exciting idea of cutting and digging my own trees left her cold. She more pragmatically pointed out that you do not buy land just to cut your own Christmas trees! I had to start all over, coming at the problem from a purely investment angle. I marshaled my figures, compared this land to other parcels we had looked at, and tried to show her that the parcel I had in mind was the better investment, all from an Analytical point of view. I also had to stress a resale for profit could be done quickly and efficiently, appealing to her Driver side. I got more of a hearing.

But rarely, outside of the immediate family, do you get a second chance to "start over." It's best to get it right the first time! Your greatest skill lies in reading your audience, appealing to the audience's values, not your own. The greatest idea, wrongly presented, equals zero in acceptance! As a supervisor of many people, your "audience" will often be thoroughly mixed, containing all the Personality Styles. As a presenter of a means-ends argument, you are going to have to present your idea from a variety of perspectives, one at a time. When you get to the point of describing the advantages of your position, be sure to show these from at least four perspectives, one each for the different Personality Styles in your immediate audience. For each Style, you will want to emphasize each of the Four Criteria a bit differently.

Bring P.A.C.E. to bear on your presentation. Your audience, the "A," is different than you, so consider what to say to the Analytic. Stress the Efficiency of your proposal and its Practicality. Anything in your proposal that does not fully account for these two Criteria will surely cause resistance from the Analytic. Show that what you propose will fit into the larger system smoothly, and accountability can be measured. With the Driver, stress Practicality and Efficacy, because he wants to do what can be done, quickly and in a down to earth manner. With the Amiable you will want to stress the people angle, showing perhaps that your idea can draw people closer together or enhance their living conditions. The Expressive wants an idea to be dramatically good and different, enhancing the image of the department or its workers.

Failure to so tailor your argument will create Constraints for you not present before you began your presentation. There are probably enough Constraints to your idea without creating additional ones because you fail to deliver your message correctly! The problem as seen by the other, the Rhetorical Problem, must be your focus as you decide how to deliver your message. Each of the Styles must be able to see their "values" inherent in your proposal. P.A.C.E. can help you analyze the upcoming encounter with your audience, and the Four Appeals can further help you decide what emphasis should be put where. The Personal Appeal, with its stress on the selfish interests of the other, you will surely want to use, but tailor it for each Style. The Four Criteria are stable and central for any Matters of Practice proposal, but your emphasis will vary as you address each Style of personality.

The larger value questions are also tremendously important. Wars have even been fought on value grounds alone. Hitler underestimated the world's response to his attempt to exterminate a segment of the German people. In his twisted and evil reasoning, the extermination policy of the Jews was Practical. He had the prisons and the railway system to hold these people. Certainly it was Efficient. What is more efficient than getting rid of people one does not like? And, it worked. Jews were killed or fled Germany. Efficacious though his policy was, it was the Value question that called the world to arms to defeat him, something he had not foreseen and clearly underestimated.

The value argument can be one of your strongest if you show that what you propose is in line with prevailing values or that your proposal will strengthen the existing value system. People want their work to mean something, to have value, so be sure to show how your means will enhance the quality of life of the department and their quality of life when off-duty.

Obviously, the best argument will show that all four Criteria are covered and accounted for, but in reality, policies and procedures often cannot make the "four star" grade. As supervisor, should you have a recommendation to make, and you cannot show all Four Criteria to be successfully met, then you must admit that, and yet argue that your proposal is worthwhile even though it may not be as Efficient or Practical as some other. YOU must say this upfront, before others attack you and point out your weakness. As you think about proposing a solution, be sure to use Empathy and sit in the chair of your antagonist. Try to anticipate his objections, and raise them first, and then show that despite such objections, your proposal has merit and is better than what is presently in place. A good tactician is never caught off guard, never surprised, so you must spend at least as much time thinking like your opponent as you do thinking like yourself!

What if one of your proposals clearly called for more paperwork by the employee, at least in the initial phases? Don't try to hide that fact, raise it, and show that although it is true your proposal may not be as economical or efficient as what is now done, nevertheless what will be gained by your means far outweighs the disadvantages. Moreover, perhaps you will argue, after the employees get used to the paperwork, they will in fact become more streamlined and efficient!

In all your proposals, using the Four Criteria to test your means-ends arguments will measurably help you present a forceful and solid argument. Not all proposals will obviously incorporate the Four Criteria. Perhaps in one or more of your proposals, for example, values do not really seem to be an issue. If so, fine, but be sure to consider whether that is really so. I have been more than once caught off guard by someone raising a value issue I had not anticipated. And, remember, although there may not be those larger societal values at issue, there will always be the values inherent in the differing Personality Styles, and these you must address!

Most important, always consider objections to your point, and raise these as part of your presentation. Then show that such objections are either not as serious as some might think, or that your proposal will in fact take care of the perceived problems. Become your worst critic. "Chameleon up" to the task of taking yourself to task before others do it for you. When you see through the eyes of your worst critic, you can set the proper context and answer the objections in your own words, in your own way. By so doing you also present the image of a fair-minded, wide-ranging thinker. Try to remain on the positive offense. Spend at least as much of your time thinking about objections to your ideas as the ideas themselves. You do not want to be caught off guard and find yourself defending every point you've made. The goal of a good presentation is to leave the listeners with nothing to say but "We agree!"

As you listen to your subordinates and colleagues present proposals, filter everything they say through the Four Criteria. Each Criterion should help you elicit good questions for the presenters. Each Criterion should provide you with a useful perspective from which to view their basic propositions. Any argument that does not take into account the Four Criteria is definitely deficient.

Where to use this heuristic? At home, to think through problems and alternatives you and your spouse face, or with your kids when they come to you with wonderful ideas about what they want to do or what the family should do. The Criteria can definitely aid you in deciding how to spend your money and your time. It is a problem-solving heuristic, a tool to use, either in listening or in advocating.

Certainly use it on the job. Much of what you do daily concerns means-ends considerations. The Four Criteria should not only be used by you, but also taught by you to your subordinates, some of who will someday become supervisors. One of the greatest gifts a supervisor can give to his people is knowledge that can further their own careers. Knowledge is power in action, and any supervisor who keeps secrets to success close to his own chest and does not pass them on to others is not only egotistical and weak, but he misses out on perhaps the greatest legacy he can leave during his tenure. The greatest supervisors we have known take real pleasure in making others successful. Helping your people become better thinkers strengthens you, for now you have better ideas coming forth to consider from below, and it strengthens your subordinates, for it gives them confidence that they can advocate good ideas and that they will have a hearing because their ideas are solidly presented. Shaping minds is one of your primary jobs. The Four Criteria is one of your best tools. Like the Four Appeals and P.A.C.E., the Four Criteria (P.E.E.V.) can make you more Consciously Competent, both in delivery and in problem-solving. Your arguments, or your responses to arguments, will be more solidly based and thorough using it! Have fun with it!

## CHAPTER FOURTEEN

# THE TACTICS OF SUPPORT: L.E.A.P.S.

N ow that you have achieved a more critical and sophisticated **rhetorical eye**, let's return to some basics of communication to ensure you are as supportive as possible when dealing with people. Some of you are already quite good at communication, so what you will find in this chapter is simply confirmation of what you already do. Others of you may have found, that despite your best intentions, you are not getting through to your people as effectively as you would like. Should this be the case, you will find this chapter extremely helpful in strengthening your entire communication repertoire.

The five basic skills or tools in communication can be defined in the acronym **L.E.A.P.S.** I have talked about these at some length in my third Book, *Verbal Judo: the Gentle Art of Persuasion* (William Morrow, 1993), but I did not apply them specifically to supervision, as we *will* now.

The "L" stands for your ability to **Listen**
The "E" for your skill in **Emphasizing** with others
The "A" for the art of **Asking** good questions
The "P" for **Paraphrase**, and
The "S" for **Summary.**

The acronym **L.E.A.P.S.** makes these skills appear sequential, but in reality they can be used, and should be used, in the order most appropriate at the time. Just remember to remain flexible throughout any communication encounter, and be prepared to shift from one tool to another as you see the need.

**Listening** is tricky business because there are four levels that constitute effective listening. First, you must be **open** to hear and understand what is being said. Sounds obvious and easy enough, but when you work with people day in and day out, you often shut down, sometimes unknowingly, and only appear to be listening. Perhaps you think you know what someone is going to say next, or perhaps you have come to gradually dislike one or more of your subordinates or colleagues so tuning them out is now the norm. Familiarity can indeed breed contempt, and sometimes the better you feel you know someone, the less closely you become inclined to listen to them. To be open, in our sense of the term, means to be unbiased and flexible. Remember "Mushin." We have learned that even the most obnoxious, irritating individual can and will say things that are worth listening to. Too many supervisors and leaders make the mistake of thinking that good ideas can't come from such people. At the same time there is a disturbing trend to ignore those in the work force and to favor those in administration. Often the people closest to the work at hand have the most accurate and workable solutions to organizational challenges.

Remember **Thompson's Law: "Look down to your people and you shall rise!"** As a preacher once said to me, "God gave you two ears and one mouth for a reason!"

Once you become open and receptive to listening to others, you then develop the skill to **hear accurately** what is being said to you. Whenever possible you should **control** your listening environment. I once had a supervisor who always talked to us on the run. "Walk with me," he would say, and I believe to this day he never really heard a thing I said. On the other hand he very well may have but his manner of listening did not convey to me that I was being heard. Here is where being attentive, regardless of your listening style, comes into play. Being **open** and making sure you **convey** you are indeed listening and hearing what is being discussed is both a sign of respect for the other party *and* perhaps the most critical factor in quality verbal communication skills.

For those who speak a second language you know how important it is to properly **interpret** what you hear. Remember that all too often people never initially say what they mean. This is a defensive tool meant to feel the other person out and to avoid confrontation, or rejection. It is not a bad or negative thing and we all employ this tactic on a daily basis. An effective listener learns to look behind the words being spoken so as to find the real message meant to be conveyed. As a supervisor, you must remember that when people talk to you they have a number of things on their minds. They have their personal needs and agenda; their team needs and agenda; their concern with how they may or may not be received; their wishes to keep or make you, their supervisor, happy.

It is not, as some poor supervisors and leaders like to promote amongst themselves, a matter of truth. It is a matter of trying to communicate in a manner that is both proactive *and* protective. Good listeners do not concern themselves with "the truth" or "the lie." They create a speaking – listening atmosphere with their subordinates that encourage openness, frankness, honesty, and respect. If someone is less than candid it will come out in such an atmosphere, especially in group discussions or meetings.

A strong supervisor will establish from the outset of his relationship with his subordinates and staff what he expects from his people. He will then enforce, and reinforce his vision. A weak leader or supervisor will do just the opposite. Subordinates fear reprisals for dissenting views if you have not made it clear from the start that you want their best perceptions. Such clarity shows your strength and helps to establish open channels of communication.

Now comes the time when you as a supervisor must *act appropriately* on what you have just heard and correctly interpreted. Acting appropriately in this case means that if you have taken someone's advice on a policy or procedure, for example, you give them due credit for their ideas and let others know of the person's contribution. Sounds obvious enough, but we have repeatedly seen good ideas taken from others with no appropriate attribution of the source and the positive impact of the idea. Good leaders and supervisors who understand the merit and benefit of proper acknowledgment keep good people in an organization. There is no point to listening, correctly interpreting, and then acting upon what you as a leader have been provided by your subordinate(s) if you are going to claim all the credit for yourself. Good employees see through this self-serving agenda and soon they stop sharing what it is they know. Why should they? There's no benefit allotted to them. However, poor employees will step forward and offer equally poor ideas and "solutions" to problems. Why? They seek to curry favor and could care less if the ego-driven agenda of their supervisor wants to claim credit. The end result of such poor leader-poor employee work relationships is obvious. The poor leader ultimately makes one mistake too many and his management demotes or replaces him. The good employee either continues working and keeping his thoughts to himself, or finds a more positive work environment and the poor employee stays right where he is and waits for another supervisory sucker to come along.

Acting appropriately also means taking action when you say you will. The **proof of quality listening lies in action taken**. Many supervisors say they listen to their people but then they take no action after all is said and done. Some supervisors or leaders are too fearful to act. Many are simply are indecisive. Taking action requires commitment and courage. It also demands total self-confidence in one's own abilities and a great commitment to "the buck stops here," if a decision turns out to be less than successful. Too many leaders and supervisors are content to let things lie, hoping others will take the lead (and the risk)! Subordinates who witness such a supervisor's inaction become discouraged. After a while, they stop suggesting; why should they? You have sent them the message and they have received it loud and clear. In creating a team the leader's challenge is to listen and then **to act** on the good advice of your subordinates. If team-driven solutions cannot be invoked, for whatever reason above your level, acting appropriately also means getting back to your employees and letting them know why you, as a team or organization, cannot necessarily move forward just yet.

Above all, the secret of good listening lies in your ability to **demonstrate by your body language that you are indeed listening!** We have all heard the communication pundits offer it is only necessary to "look" as if you are listening to someone. Wrong answer! People will detect this form of physical deception sooner or later, and when they do you will lose any and all respect from them from that point on. The quality leader or supervisor truly wants to, indeed needs to, listen to his people. He will demonstrate that he is doing so by his body language as well as by his responses. If you do not have the time, or the energy to provide a proper setting for discussion then tell the employee or subordinate so. Make a date! Make an appointment! Ask them to come back later that afternoon when you are free! People respect honesty and they will respect you for telling them you want quality time to hear what they have to say. There is another benefit to this course of action, those employees or subordinates who simply talk-talk-talk will most often not bother you again if you dictate the time and place of further conversation. They are impulse-driven communicators and, once they realize their impulse to talk to you will not be rewarded with an immediate audience, they will lose interest and flutter off to find someone else with nothing better to do than have their ear bent.

Remember, if you fake listening it'll catch up to you and the cost is enormous. Be a considerate listener, and a wise one. Control the time, the space, and the environment for quality discussion and listening. Defer to the employee or subordinate who respects this approach, and dissuade the impulse communicator who just wants a handy sounding board.

The **"E"** stands for **Empathize**. Good communication begins and ends with seeing things as your people see them. When in doubt, stand in the shoes of your subordinate or employee. If you follow the **"Hook-Down" Tactic** we discussed earlier, you will find empathy an easy tool to employ. Remember, empathy is not sympathy. You do not have to like or feel for others, but you should make a good faith effort to understand their side of the fence. Once you know how others are thinking and feeling, you can more skillfully construct a verbal means to relate to them in a positive, proactive manner. The most often-heard complaint we hear from workers across the board is they feel their bosses have lost touch with them and the work they do. And in too many cases they are right! Your strength as a leader or supervisor is anchored in your people believing you are with them, although a level (or several) above them management wise. Create this bridge and half your battles will be won right off the bat.

For example, while in northern Iraq on a civilian protection project my co-author spent his first two days meeting with his team of U.S. advisors. They were in a remote location, working long hours, had few resources, and the environment was exceptionally risky. After meeting and listening with his team, then working with them on solutions to the many challenges they'd brought up, he offered to work a day out "on the line" with them. At first the group offered because Greg was their boss he could do as he pleased; they did not expect him to do anything more than what he'd already done. However, Greg knew that simply listening, taking notes, and offering a motivational speech to such a team was not enough. He needed to subordinate himself to the team and do what it was they were doing daily.

So the next day he clambered up atop a roof and for the next seven hours pulled watch with a borrowed rifle along with another member of the resident team. Despite 120-degree heat and no shade, Greg pulled his watch just like any other member of the team. At the end of the day, when all returned to the air-conditioned barracks, his relationship as both a boss and as an operator was cemented in place. He'd talked the talk and then walked the walk. Better, he'd demonstrated his professional trust in the team and its leadership by subordinating his clearly understood role as their boss to that of the team's leadership. And over the course of the day he'd been able to observe firsthand and listen to how the team worked with each other and those others they necessarily had to interact with, which helped him support the observations and recommendations he would later make to his upper management on how to better support and refine the project's worth.

> *Listening, and then doing, are critical functions of the professional leader or supervisor. Failure at either means failure overall.* —Thompson's Law.

The **"A"** stands for **Ask**, your critical ability to ask good questions to elicit good information. There are five basic types of questions you can ask others, and each has a different psychological effect on your audience. Let's look at these now.

First, there are **fact-finding** questions. These are questions normally the most important to you as a leader or supervisor. You need the correct answers to these questions to do your job. Fact-finding questions are fairly straightforward and most of us are fairly good at asking them already. However, we recommend **never asking these when people are upset**! Why? Because angry people giving responses to such questions when they are indeed upset will almost often provide emotionally and traumatically colored data. Corrupted data is bad data and bad data equals wrong answers to real problems or challenges. Again, control the atmosphere and environment of the listening process and you will avoid this pitfall.

Second, there are **general questions,** which by their very nature are open-ended. The openness of the general question gives freedom to the responder. The fact-finding question calls for specific data: "What caused the system to shut down?" The general question on the same subject might be "Have we had similar problems with this system in the recent past?" Psychologically, general questions are good because they relax a person and allow him to gradually expand on what you need or want to know. General questions are vanilla; they almost make you, the leader/supervisor, appear the one at a loss. This encourages the employee, subordinate, or even family member to want to demonstrate their expertise, knowledge, or wish to help you understand. Start off in general and work toward the specific, or fact-finding category of question. This one-two punch is a nice combination and raises little resistance if done right.

The third type of question is the **direct question**. Direct questions require direct answers. "Can we finish this repair by 1600 today?" is a direct question. This category of question is effective for getting clear-cut, timely information. However you must sense the timing for asking such a question, based on the atmosphere, environment, state of mind of the person you are asking, and your own need for the information you hope to obtain. Supervisors who only ask direct questions are often given shallow responses, or responses that err on the side of the person being asked. There is a time and a place for a direct question, as any good and successful parent will attest to. There is also a time to elicit the same information by combining a general, and then fact-finding, then direct question sequence, if you truly want the best range of answer possible.

**Leading questions,** so defined because you literally put words in the mouths of others, are the most 'iffy' questions you can ask. "If we wanted to complete the project by tomorrow wouldn't it be okay to cut this corner just a hair today?" is such a question. The weak employee or subordinate is encouraged to answer in the affirmative for what should now be apparent reasons. The strong employee or subordinate will have little room to discuss the better alternative as you, the question asker and management figure, have sent the message you want by asking the question the way you did. Avoid leading questions whenever possible, or catch yourself when asking them and rephrase the thought. There's a reason trial lawyers object to such questions in court, and why such questions are struck down by the presiding judge. The answers to leading questions are contained in the question itself, and most always they are subjective as opposed to objective, at best.

A leading question in an interview can be useful when you are trying to find out something from a difficult employee or subordinate, and you are 90 percent sure of your facts and are looking for that last 10% to be dead certain. And, they are necessary under emergency conditions where you are the expert and the respondent needs your direction. We teach this technique to 911 dispatchers who have to lead emotionally overwrought callers to provide the crucial information to get them the appropriate help they need.

Finally, the **opinion-seeking** question, those wonderful "what would you have me do" question. This category of question is meant to encourage positive interaction between a supervisor and a subordinate. Most people value being asked such a question; all people feel better when asked such a question even if they don't have a ready answer; and all people feel empowered by you, the leader or supervisor, when asked this category of question. The problem is that too many supervisors use the opinion-seeking question to turn the tables on their employees. Again from my co-author's experience:

> *Greg related going to his general manager during one contract in Iraq and asking for some specific guidance and direction on an area important to the company he was charged with managing at the time. In response, the general manager offered Greg should seek his own answers, in his own way, based on his own opinions and perceptions of the problem and that he (the general manager) was comfortable with this solution. In short, the general manager didn't want to take responsibility for any upper management guidance or direction and used the opinion-seeking question to evade executing his responsibility, to provide help to one of his subordinates. Leaders and supervisors who quietly seek to evade the responsibility of their positions will corrupt the opinion-seeking question to do just this—put the onus of responsibility back on the one seeking help. It is a cheap, pathetic, transparent ploy and management personnel who employ it are a discredit to their organizations and ultimately cost everyone involved time, money, and positive forward momentum.*

Now that you have these five categories of questions clearly in mind, let us offer you two strategies to use in your questioning. First, always seek to **forecast** or set the context before you begin your questioning. Explain to your audience the direction you will be taking and the purpose of the questioning. This approach calms people down and prepares them to be good respondents. You 'prime the pump' for voluntary compliance. If you don't do this, people will often tighten up on you, as they try to guess where you are going and what all these questions are really about. Forecasting is another way of showing respect for your audience—you care enough to let them in on what you are doing—and tactically you are making them better at giving you the information you need. And finally, to have to forecast forces you to frame your questions in some meaningful, tactical order, so it is good for you, too!

Second, always **vary your questions!** Too many of any one category of question causes problems. Too many fact-finding or direct questions closes people down because they feel they are being attacked. Too many general or opinion-seeking questions can make you look weak or indecisive. As a rule of thumb, switch up whenever you sense resistance in answering. The two categories of question that have the most positive effect on an audience are the **general** and the **opinion-seeking**; the two most potentially negative are the **direct** and the **leading** questions. Watch your audience carefully and be flexible with your questions. Sometimes it's best to simply stop asking questions and to ask for a glass of water.

The **"P"** stands for **Paraphrase,** the most powerful of the tools noted. We have discussed this at some length in Chapter Four, and I have discussed at length the 14 advantages to paraphrase in my third book, *Verbal Judo: the Gentle Art of Persuasion,* Chapter 10. But we do wish to stress several of these advantages for you the supervisor.

Remember, paraphrase is putting the other's perceived meaning into your words. The moment you begin to paraphrase, the other begins to listen because, after all, you are talking about **his ideas!** Hence, using paraphrase makes people better listeners! As the other listens hearing his meaning come back in your calmer, more professional language motivates him **to modify** his original, possibly extreme statements, thus allowing him to restate his meaning and not lose personal face!

Paraphrase also overcomes an interesting phenomenon known as **sonic intention.** People often think they have said something to you because they have "heard" themselves rehearse it in their minds. When you paraphrase, they hear what you have heard, not what they think they have said, and this can end miscommunication errors. Understanding sonic intention will ensure you do not make severe errors when taking direction from superiors. Use paraphrase yourself to ensure you have heard and interpreted the other's intended meaning. Your supervisor, for example, may have thought he told you to get a report to him no later than the 15$^{th}$ at 1pm sharp, but in fact he only said "no later than the 15$^{th}$." Should you fail to paraphrase him at the moment of taking direction, and you leave his office, later putting your report on his desk at 3 p.m. on the 15$^{th}$, he will say, "But I told you 1 p.m. sharp! I needed it for a meeting at 1:15 p.m. so your information wasn't included."

The only way to have protected yourself was to have used paraphrase earlier: "Ok, let me be sure I understand what I am to do. You want me to research X topic and you need my report no later than the 15$^{th}$? Yes?" Your supervisor, having now heard back what you first heard from him, can now correct the initial miscommunication by saying, "And no later than 1 p.m. or your work cannot be used." Remember, if the supervisor believes he said it, he said it! As a supervisor you can use this same simple tool by encouraging your subordinates to repeat back to you what you have just said. This opens the door to continued two-way communication that is accurate, and it encourages the employee to take notes, listen closely, and be accurate. You may call on him!

Finally, we need to become experts at **Summary** the "S" in LEAPS. Summary means to condense all that has gone before into one brief statement of accurate meaning and intent. There are two specific uses for summary. As a leader/supervisor we use it to **voice decisions**. Once you have listened, emphasized, asked, and paraphrased, you must prepare to make a decision, and the very utterance of a decision should sound different than anything that preceded it. As a communication tactic, **Summary** creates decisiveness and authority, **if you verbalize it correctly**. A decision statement must have three qualities: brevity, clarity, and right tone for the atmosphere or environment. People must know you are voicing a decisive statement. Your decisive statement must exude your supervisory authority and will. As such, then, such a summary statement must be **brief**, long statements lose their force, and it must be so **clear** the least capable subordinate can grasp what you want done.

**Summary** can and should also be used whenever you find you have been interrupted in speaking with someone. **Summary reconnects communication** that has been interrupted, and we call this technique the **"fish-hook"** tactic. In this modern age of ceaseless movement and noise, we often are interrupted in the middle of a dialogue with another. **Thompson's Law:**

*"Once interrupted, never pick up where you left off, but employ the fish-hook of summary!"*

Example, you are talking on the phone and you have to put someone on hold to talk on a second line. When you come back to the first caller, don't just continue where you left off, for the other's mind has drifted, as has yours with the second caller. Instead, re-hook the first caller by using a short piece of summary, such as, "Ok, we were just discussing A and B, is that correct?" When he affirms this to be the case, or corrects you, continue the discussion. In this way you nicely hook back into where you had to leave off, and you are back in control of the discussion.

**L.E.A.P.S.**, then, represents the five tactical skills necessary to interact with people with effectiveness and respect. You already employ these tactics on a daily basis, but being **consciously competent** regarding the power of each, can measurably improve the chances of you using these under pressure effectively. As a supervisor, use these skills and tactics, but as important, teach them to your staff. Model good communication, and then pass the secret on to others. Miscommunication only exists because we think it is a natural, easy-occurring phenomenon. It is not. It is an artificial, tactic skill. Question thoughtfully using the categories we have discussed, and always summarize so the final message is clear, concise, and doable by those charged to make things happen on your behalf.

## CHAPTER FIFTEEN

# LEADERSHIP AND THE ROLE OF TRAINING

R ealistic, concurrent, ongoing professional training is the hallmark of the Professional. As a capable, effective, respected supervisor and leader, you will want to leave your mark on your organization when you either retire or move on in your career. Rest assured your legacy is today being fashioned by how you treat, develop, mentor, manage, lead and train your people. Well-trained employees or subordinates are capable, profitable, reliable assets. Untrained, or worse yet, poorly trained people are exactly the opposite.

Training your organization's people is one of the most important tasks and leadership responsibilities you will have as a supervisor. And to properly train people you must be able to properly communicate with them.

Verbal communications skills must be a part of any organization's quest for excellence. As such, these must be organized, developed, trained and then reinforced/rewarded by you as a leader. But before you can accomplish this necessary task you must first "walk the walk" when it comes to talking the talk. Frankly, it's been my personal experience as founder and developer of the Verbal Judo program, that where many, many police departments, for example, take advantage of sending their staffs and officers to our courses, the reality is that once back in the office or on the street it's "business as usual" where verbal communication goes. This is simply poor leadership from the top down where enhancing the employee body is concerned, and a waste of public funds from my point of view. Leaders ensure that the training they approve, fund, and provide is followed up on, made part of the institution, and constantly promoted as "the way to do things right."

There are fortunately many law enforcement leaders and supervisors who understand this critical component to success but certainly not enough. There are likewise many proactive, positive, selfless business, military, and community leaders throughout our great country who daily commit themselves and their organizations to doing the hard right over the easy wrong, and who then provide the appropriate training to make sure this necessary goal will be accomplished and then taken to the next level.

**Right leadership** is what Verbal Judo is all about. And to reach right leadership we believe you must be able to communicate correctly, accurately, and in-synch with all those whom you come into contact with daily as a leader, a manager, or a supervisor. This book is about just this: communicating as a leader in a manner that assures success for you, your employees, and your organization and to whomever it may be ultimately responsible.

We close with this story about how sound verbal communications and leadership training can save lives.

One afternoon, several years ago, my co-author was one of three officers called to assist in a health and welfare check. The subject, a woman with a nursing degree and background, was reported by her doctor to be taking anti-depressant medication and drinking, a potent chemical mix. When the officers arrived, the woman opened the door to her home, walked back to her bedroom, and produced a .38 caliber revolver. She then threatened to kill either the officers or herself if they did not leave the premises.

For nearly 45 minutes the officers worked diligently together as a team to try to bring the event to a successful close. They obeyed the woman's impaired commands and directives as appropriate; they engaged her in conversation, asking questions from categories of questions covered in this book; they communicated carefully and accurately with each other, and with all those outside agencies and service providers necessary in such a dangerous situation. However, no matter what they did they could not get the woman to put down her gun.

Finally, all negotiations came to a stop. The woman began screaming at the officers to leave her home. As she did so she began storming down a short hallway at them, her revolver held in both hands at chest level, her finger on the trigger. Two officers were able to leave the house safely, the third – Greg – was confronted in the living room by the woman. A weapon-to-weapon standoff between the two ensued. According to my co-author, now facing a clearly suicidal suspect with the means, intent, and opportunity to use her weapon against him, it was his previous communications training that saved the day.

For three or four crucial minutes Greg continued talking with the woman. Even when she began screaming, *"You better kill me or I'm going to kill you!"* he managed to maintain his professional calm and resolution. For the past 45 minutes he listened to the woman tell her story; he'd qualified her as a normally responsible person; he'd asked her questions and he'd gotten the answers he needed; he'd given her time, space, and respect. He'd impressed upon her that he was there to help, not hurt. There to resolve problems, not make more of them. He was there as a friend, not as an enemy.

Continuing to talk, to communicate, and to work with the woman, he successfully brought the situation to a critical moment. She agreed to point her weapon in a safe direction so he could voluntarily comply with her demand he leave the house. Before doing so he'd reinforced to her that he would not kill her and that it was his professional belief that as a nurse, she would not harm him. "The entire time we as a team of officers were talking with her I'd come to the conclusion she was first and foremost in great pain for herself," Greg recalls. "She was a trauma nurse so I knew she was in the business of saving lives, not taking them. She was intent on perhaps dying at the moment, but it was she who wanted to die, not anyone else. It was a calculated risk on my part as I could have shot and killed her right there, we were within feet of each other at the time, but my training and experience both as a Special Forces operator and police officer allowed that sixth sense we all have to affirm to me no one had to die that day."

In the end Greg left the house. While doing so the woman was distracted for a split second and a second officer, the patrol sergeant on duty, saw his chance. He rushed through the front door and tackled the woman. Both line officers turned and rushed in behind their supervisor, and although the woman managed to fire all five bullets each only penetrated the living room rug, as my co-author had obtained control of the gun and held the weapon in place as she emptied it into her carpet.

A short time later, while awaiting booking downtown, the woman told then Officer Walker "I never would have harmed you...I am just in so much pain I want to die." She would later plead guilty to a number of charges, and during sentencing thanked the officers present that day for not taking her life.

Today that officer, my co-author, credits the successful and happy ending to what could have been a tragedy for all to his professional training in proper verbal communications skills.

"Over the course of nearly 30 years of work, law enforcement or otherwise, it was the rock solid foundation of my training across the board that allowed what happened to occur. Training, *right* training, made the difference between life and death. And right leadership, as exhibited that day by our patrol sergeant, took correct advantage of that training and we, as a team, eventually saved that woman's life."

**Right Leadership. Right Communication. Right Training.** We believe these three pillars of Professional Excellence are what make the difference in today's world. The ancient Chinese general Sun-Tzu offers: *the ultimate form of combat is overpowering one's enemy without fighting.*

With **Verbal Judo Leadership** this truth can and is being achieved every day by true law enforcement leaders and supervisors—WOOSHA!

# INDEX

5-Step Tactic .................................................. 126
Art of persuasion ............................................ 36
Art of Representation ....................................... 50
    Figure Eight ............................................. 50, 51
Ask .............................................................. 166
Body language ............................................... 64, 65
Broken rhythm .............................................. 142, 143
Chain of Command ......................................... 33
Code of Silence .............................................. 20
Communication profile .................................... 83, 85
    amiable .................................................... 94
    analytic ................................................... 94
    cross-quadrants ....................................... 98
    driver ..................................................... 93
    expressive ............................................... 95
Compliance; voluntary .................................... 33
Conscious competent ...................... 77, 80, 81, 84
Conscious incompetent .................................... 78
Contact power ............................................... 76
Contact Professional ...................................... 53
Continuity of Confusion .................................. 26
Distance and separation .................................. 76
Effectiveness
    content .................................................... 61
    tone ....................................................... 61
    voice ...................................................... 61
Empathize .................................................... 165
Ethical appeal ............................................... 133, 140
Ethical Presence ............................................ 26, 151
Ethics/Values ................................................ 15, 17, 20
Extended street experience .............................. 11
Field Training Officer ..................................... 12
Five Steps .................................................... 125
Five-Step Hard Style ...................................... 153
Five-Step Hard Style matrix ............................ 36
    act ......................................................... 40
    ask ........................................................ 36

confirmation ......................................................................... 40

options ................................................................................ 37

set the context ................................................................... 36

Force Options ......................................................... 34, 41

presence ............................................................................. 34

words .................................................................................. 36

FTO programs ........................................................................ 11

Golden Rule of the Street ..................................................... 48

Hook Down Principle ............................................................. 77

Hook Down theory ................................................... 69, 83, 110

Intervention

advanced ............................................................................ 25

delayed ............................................................................... 25

immediate ......................................................................... 21

L.E.A.P.S. ................................................................... 161, 171

Leadership ........................................................................... viii

Leading questions ............................................................... 167

Listening ............................................................................. 161

Management tactics ............................................................... 2

Mushin ...................................................................... 42, 47, 121

Other Non-Verbals (ONVs) ................................................... 64

P.A.C.E. ...................................................... 145, 151, 157

P.E.E.V. ............................................................................... 154

P.O.S.T. ................................................................................. 21

Paraphrase .......................................................................... 169

Personal Appeal .................................................. 111, 139, 140

Police management ................................................................. 8

Practical Appeal ............................................................ 141, 142

Praise; art of ....................................................................... 113

Principle of supervision ...................................................... 105

Quality Contact .................................................................... 33

Rational Appeal ................................................................... 137

Real Self ............................................................................... 59

Resolution ............................................................................ 124

Right leadership .................................................................. 174

Self as Seen by Others .................................................. 60, 66

Self as Seen by the Self ....................................................... 60

Specific behavior ................................................................. 123

Street truths ......................................................................... 55

Summary .............................................................................. 170

Supervision .......................................................................... 31

Sword of Interruption ............................................................ 57
Tactical Empathy .......................................................... 140, 141
Thompson's Law .................................................................. 118
Unconscious competent ...................................................... 79, 80
Unconscious incompetent ......................................................... 77
Verbal communications skills ................................................... 173
Verbal deflection .................................................................. 47
Voice; elements of
    modulation ..................................................................... 63
    pace ............................................................................. 63
    pitch ............................................................................ 63

# COMMUNICATION PROFILE SURVEY (PULL-OUT)

The following survey is designed to assist you in identifying and describing the underlying strengths you use in your relationships with other people. You are presented with a number of self-descriptive statements, each of which is followed by four different endings. You are to indicate the order in which you feel each ending is characteristic of yourself.

In the space provided by each response, fill in the numbers

4   for **most** like you,      3   for **next most** like you,
2   for **less like you**, and  1   for **least like you**.

Fill in **all** blanks for each question, and each question will have 4, 3, 2, or 1. Leave *nothing blank* and do not repeat any number.

**NOTE:** Answer these questions quickly and naturally. Answer them as you see yourself. Too much thought—**No Good! Be Honest!**

1.  **I am likely to impress others as...**
    _____a. practical and to the point.
    _____b. emotional and somewhat stimulating.
    _____c. astute and logical.
    _____d. intellectually oriented and somewhat complex.

2.  **In the way I work on projects, I may ...**
    _____a. want it to be stimulating and involve lively interaction with others.
    _____b. concentrate to make sure the project is systematically or logically developed.
    _____c. want to be sure the project has a tangible "pay off" that will justify spending my time and energy on it.
    _____d. be most concerned as to whether the project "breaks ground" for advanced knowledge.

3.  **In communicating with others, I may...**
    _____a. express unintended boredom with talk that is too detailed.
    _____b. convey impatience with those who express ideas that are not thought through.
    _____c. show little interest in thoughts and ideas that show little or no originality.
    _____d. tend to ignore those who talk about "long range implicators" and direct my attention to what needs to be done right now.

4. **When confronted by others with a different point of view, I usually make progress by...**

_____a. getting at least one or two specific commitments on which we can "build" later.

_____b. trying to place myself in "the shoes of others."

_____c. keeping my composure and helping others to see things simply and logically.

_____d. relying on my basic ability to conceptualize and pull ideas together.

5. **In terms of time, I probably concentrate most on...**

_____a. whether what I am doing or planning to do is going to hurt or disturb others.

_____b. making sure that any actions I take are consistent and part of a systematic progression.

_____c. my immediate actions and involvements, and whether they make sense today.

_____d. significant long-range actions I plan to take and how they relate to my life's direction.

6. **In reaction to individuals whom I meet socially, I am likely to consider...**

_____a. they contribute ideas and challenges.

_____b. they seem thoughtful and reflective.

_____c. they are interesting and fun to be with.

_____d. they know what they are doing and can get things done.

7. **I feel satisfied with myself when I...**

_____a. get more things accomplished than I planned.

_____b. comprehend the underlying feelings of others and react in a helpful way.

_____c. solve a problem by using a logical or systematic method.

_____d. develop new thoughts or ideas, which can be related.

8. **I find it easy to be convincing when I am...**

_____a. in touch with my own feelings and those of others.

_____b. logical, patient and forbearing.

_____c. down to earth and to the point.

_____d. intellectually on top of things and take all relevant factors into account.

9. **I enjoy it when others see me as...**

_____a. intellectually gifted and having vision.

_____b. an individual who knows where he is going and has the ability to get there.

_____c. creative and stimulating.

_____d. a dependable individual who gets things done and always "comes through."

10. **When circumstances prevent me from doing what I want, I find it useful to...**

_____a. review any deficiencies or "soft spots" in my approach and modify accordingly.

_____b. review all that has happened and develop a new hypothesis or model for action.

_____c. keep in mind the basics, pinpoint the key obstacle(s), and modify my game plan to take these into account.

_____d. analyze the motivation of others and develop a new "feel" for the situation.

11. **Sometimes I suspect I may come across to others as being...**

_____a. too emotional or too intense.

_____b. almost too controlled or perhaps too logical.

_____c. too concerned with specifics and matters related to "the how to."

_____d. overly wrapped up in ideas and somewhat hard "to read."

12. **When I write business correspondence to someone I do not know, I usually try to ...**

_____a. clarify the background reasons for the contact and relate this to my purpose in writing.

_____b. highlight in plain language what I want, need, or expect of the other.

_____c. show how my main points fit into a broader perspective.

_____d. convey at least some information about my style and myself.

13. **In speaking before groups with whom I have little regular contact, I like to leave the impression of being...**

_____a. a systematic thinker who can analyze the kind of problems the particular group is concerned about.

_____b. a broad-gauge thinker capable of making some innovative contribution.

_____c. a practical and resourceful person who could help the group define its concerns and who can assist in solving its problems.

_____d. lively and impactful person who was clearly "in touch" with their mood and needs.

14. **In tense meetings with others, I may occasionally...**

_____a. let "my hair down" too freely, expressing feelings which might have been better left unsaid.

_____b. be overly cautious and avoid some contacts which might have proved rewarding.

_____c. miss the "forest for the trees," become so concerned with a given facet of a person that I fail to see other, less obvious important characteristics.

_____d. be swayed by others who are gifted but perhaps lacking direction.

**15. If I am not careful, others may at times feel that I am...**

_____a. highly unemotional and inclined toward being impersonal or detached.

_____b. plodding, superficial, or self-centered.

_____c. somewhat snobbish, intellectual superior or condescending.

_____d. moody, excitable, or unpredictable.

**16. When "the chips are down," I feel it is preferable to...**

_____a. stick to a systematic approach that has proven effective before, even though by taking more risks I might win a few more victories.

_____b. be respected as original even if it costs me something in the short run.

_____c. concentrate on getting what I want accomplished right now even if such an approach lacks dramatic impact.

_____d. be spontaneous and say what I really think.

**17. When others pressure me I am...**

_____a. overly emotional, impulsive, or apt to get "carried away" by my feelings.

_____b. too inclined toward being analytical and critical of them.

_____c. too concerned with proving myself with immediate action.

_____d. inclined to step back into my own world of thoughts.

**18. In considering my approach to difficult situations, it is possible that I become overly-involved...**

_____a. in a battle of wits and problem solving, even for their own sake.

_____b. in the immediate here and now, getting and doing as I wish.

_____c. in the world of concepts, values, and ideas.

_____d. about the feelings of others.

## Scoring and Evaluation

Fill in the following chart. There are 18 responses. To the right of each, there are four blanks identified by letters. These represent your responses for each question. Fill in the blanks with the number you put for each letter. Note that the letters are in mixed order, so be careful. When you have completed the first 9, total each column and put the total on the line provided. Reading across, these should add up to 90. Do the same for the last nine. These, too, should add up to 90 reading across.

| RESPONSE | EXP | AN | AM | D |
|---|---|---|---|---|
| 1. | d. _____ | c._____ | b. _____ | a. _____ |
| 2. | d. _____ | b. _____ | a. _____ | c. _____ |
| 3. | a. _____ | b. _____ | c. _____ | d. _____ |
| 4. | d. _____ | c. _____ | b. _____ | a. _____ |
| 5. | d. _____ | b._____ | a. _____ | c. _____ |
| 6. | a. _____ | b. _____ | c. _____ | d. _____ |
| 7. | d. _____ | c. _____ | b. _____ | a. _____ |
| 8. | d. _____ | b. _____ | a. _____ | c. _____ |
| 9. | a. _____ | b. _____ | c. _____ | d. _____ |
| | _____ | _____ | _____ | _____ = 90 |

Top Score

| | | | | |
|---|---|---|---|---|
| 10. | b. _____ | a. _____ | d. _____ | c. _____ |
| 11. | d. _____ | b. _____ | a. _____ | c. _____ |
| 12. | c. _____ | a. _____ | d. _____ | b. _____ |
| 13. | b. _____ | a. _____ | d. _____ | c. _____ |
| 14. | d. _____ | b. _____ | a. _____ | c. _____ |
| 15. | c. _____ | a, _____ | d. _____ | b. _____ |
| 16. | b. _____ | a. _____ | d. _____ | c. _____ |
| 17. | d. _____ | b. _____ | a. _____ | c. _____ |
| 18. | c. _____ | a. _____ | d. _____ | b. _____ |
| | _____ | _____ | _____ | _____ = 90 |

Bottom score:

**Path of the Warrior**
*An Ethical Guide to Personal & Professional
Development in the Field of Criminal Justice*
by Larry F. Jetmore

**The COMPSTAT Paradigm**
*Management Accountability in Policing, Business and
the Public Sector*
by Vincent E. Henry, CPP, Ph.D.

**The New Age of Police Supervision and Management**
*A Behavioral Concept*
by Michael A. Petrillo & Daniel R. DelBagno

**Effective Police Leadership - 2nd Edition**
*Moving Beyond Management*
by Thomas E. Baker, Lt. Col. MP USAR (Ret.)

**The Lou Savelli Pocketguides -**

*Gangs Across America and Their Symbols*
*Identity Theft - Understanding and Investigation*
*Guide for the War on Terror*
*Basic Crime Scene Investigation*
*Graffiti*
*Street Drugs Identification*
*Cop Jokes*
*Practical Spanish for LEOs*

**(800) 647-5547        www.LooseleafLaw.com**